P9-ARM-853

BREAKING INTO THE GAME INDUSTRY: ADVICE FOR A SUCCESSFUL CAREER FROM THOSE WHO HAVE DONE IT

BRENDA BRATHWAITE
IAN SCHREIBER

Course Technology PTR
A part of Cengage Learning

COURSE TECHNOLOGY
CENGAGE Learning

Australia • Brazil • Japan • Korea • Mexico • Singapore • Spain • United Kingdom • United States

NEW ENGLAND INSTITUTE OF TECHNOLOGY
LIBRARY

11-11   #743292289

COURSE TECHNOLOGY
CENGAGE Learning·

Breaking into the Game Industry: Advice for a Successful Career from Those Who Have Done It
Brenda Brathwaite and Ian Schreiber

Publisher and General Manager, Course Technology PTR: Stacy L. Hiquet

Associate Director of Marketing:
Sarah Panella

Manager of Editorial Services:
Heather Talbot

Marketing Manager: Jordan Castellani

Acquisitions Editor: Heather Hurley

Project/Copy Editor: Kezia Endsley

Interior Layout Tech: MPS Limited,
a Macmillan Company

Cover Designer: Mike Tanamachi

Indexer: Larry Sweazy

Proofreader: Melba Hopper

© 2012 Course Technology, a part of Cengage Learning.

ALL RIGHTS RESERVED. No part of this work covered by the copyright herein may be reproduced, transmitted, stored, or used in any form or by any means graphic, electronic, or mechanical, including but not limited to photocopying, recording, scanning, digitizing, taping, Web distribution, information networks, or information storage and retrieval systems, except as permitted under Section 107 or 108 of the 1976 United States Copyright Act, without the prior written permission of the publisher.

For product information and technology assistance, contact us at
Cengage Learning Customer & Sales Support, 1-800-354-9706

For permission to use material from this text or product,
submit all requests online at **www.cengage.com/permissions**
Further permissions questions can be emailed to
permissionrequest@cengage.com

All trademarks are the property of their respective owners.

All images © Cengage Learning unless otherwise noted.

Library of Congress Control Number: 2011926538

ISBN-13: 978-1-4354-5804-8

ISBN-10: 1-4354-5804-4

Course Technology, a part of Cengage Learning
20 Channel Center Street
Boston, MA 02210
USA

Cengage Learning is a leading provider of customized learning solutions with office locations around the globe, including Singapore, the United Kingdom, Australia, Mexico, Brazil, and Japan. Locate your local office at: **international.cengage.com/region**

Cengage Learning products are represented in Canada by Nelson Education, Ltd.

For your lifelong learning solutions, visit **courseptr.com**

Visit our corporate website at **cengage.com**

Printed in the United States of America
1 2 3 4 5 6 7 13 12 11

ACKNOWLEDGMENTS

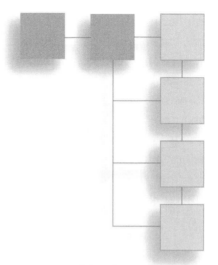

This book is the result of the experience of a great many friends in the game industry who have shared their generous advice and a space with us in this wonderful community. Thanks is also due to the many people hoping to enter the game industry who have asked us the questions which, once answered again and again, became the inspiration for this book. Thanks, too, to the Game Developers Conference, which provided the venue for Brenda's lecture, "100 Questions, 97 Answers, and 56 Minutes." It served as the verbal outline for this book. Thank you, everyone, for your help in pulling this massive work together.

Brenda: In addition to everyone included above, five people fill my life with games and love. My kids—Maezza, Avalon, and Donovan—all want to be game designers and coders in the game industry. Their newfound passion for this amazing medium constantly reignites my own. I am also deeply inspired by my longtime friend and love, John Romero, for being a living, walking, breathing bible of gameplay, game design, and coding knowledge, and love and inspiration. To have that kind of genius in my world all the time is nothing short of a miracle. Like my own children, John's son Michael, now in his second year in the industry, shares our deep love of games and provides a great role model for everyone, but especially my kids, who want to pursue the dream. My thanks also go out to Nasir Gebelli and Bill Budge who serve as the founding fathers of the computer game industry. Everywhere I go, every legendary designer and coder I talk to, they mention Gebelli or Budge (and sometimes both) as their foundation. Without them, without players, without my family, without you, my world would not be the beautiful place it is today. Thank you.

Ian: For me, I have had so many influences that it is impossible to list everyone here, but above all I must thank my soul mate and life partner Sharon for her love, support, and patience during the course of writing this book. Also to my daughter Janis for enabling me to view the world in completely different ways that will ultimately make me a better designer. I'm also grateful for my parents, who always encouraged me to go after my dreams, whether or not my dreams were lucrative. Finally, I wish to thank anyone, anywhere, who has designed and shipped a game; the best games inspire me to improve my skills so I can make something as good, while the worst games inspire me to get out there and prove that I can make something better.

Have fun.

About the Authors

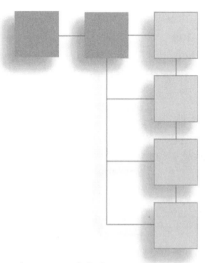

Brenda Brathwaite (1981, COO and Game Designer, Loot Drop) is an award-winning game designer, artist, writer, and creative director who entered the video game industry in 1981 at the age of 15. Brenda has worked with a variety of companies, including Atari, Sir-tech Software, Electronic Arts, Firaxis, and numerous companies in the social media space. Before founding Loot Drop, Brathwaite served as Creative Director for two social media companies—Slide (acquired by Google) and Lolapps. She has worked on many Facebook games with DAUs in the millions, including *Ravenwood Fair, Critter Island, SuperPoke Pets!, SPP Ranch, Garden Life, Rock Riot,* and *Top Fish.*

Brenda served on the board of the International Game Developers Association (IGDA) and presently chairs the IGDA's Women in Games Special Interest group. She also served on the advisory board for the Smithsonian's video game history exhibition and the International Center for the History of Electronic Games at the Strong Museum of Play.

She was named Woman of the Year by *Charisma+2 Magazine* in 2010 and also was a nominee in Microsoft's 2010 Women in Games game design awards. In 2009, her game *Train* won the coveted Vanguard Award at IndieCade for "pushing the boundaries of game design and showing us what games can do." She was named one of the top 20 most influential women in the game industry by

Gamasutra.com in 2008 and one of the 100 most influential women in the game industry by *Next Generation* magazine in 2007. *Nerve* magazine also called her one of the 50 artists, actors, authors, activists, and icons who are making the world a more stimulating place.

Ian Schreiber (2000, Programmer/Game Designer/ Teacher, Freelance) has worked on seven shipped games, including online trading card games, console games, and even some "serious games" for corporate training. He has consulted on a variety of additional titles, which he can't tell you about since he's under NDA (see Question 69).

Ian has also taught college students how to make games since 2006. He has worked with two-year and four-year colleges and universities, both in person and online, teaching classes, created course content, and consulting for curriculum development.

Ian is a co-founder of the Global Game Jam, the world's largest game creation event. Other than that, he does not have nearly the impressive credentials that Brenda has, but that has not stopped him from managing to work with Brenda on this book and many other projects.

CONTENTS

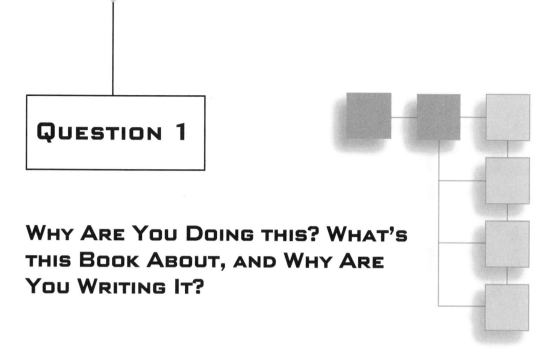

QUESTION 1

WHY ARE YOU DOING THIS? WHAT'S THIS BOOK ABOUT, AND WHY ARE YOU WRITING IT?

Brenda: Hi. My name is Brenda Brathwaite, and I've been in the game industry since 1982 when I was just 15 years old. I've been making games ever since. During that time, I've just about seen it all. I've helped a lot of people break in, helped a few break out, and have been asked thousands of questions. This book is about the 100 most common questions I am asked. I'm writing it with the aid of co-conspirator, game designer, programmer, and educator Ian Schreiber. Like me, Ian's spent a good number of years in the industry and has answered many of these questions dozens of times, too.

Our opinions, however, are just that—opinions. Our experience is singular and not applicable to everyone. That's why I've invited hundreds of my closest friends to chime in with their opinions. Sometimes they are in resounding agreement with one another, but other times, their opinions resemble night and day. For each opinion, we list the name and current job title of the person, along with the year they started working in the game industry.

Feel free to hop around the book and find answers to the questions you have. There's no specific order to the questions, but some are grouped together for logic's sake. Flip through the table of contents and find the sections or questions that are of the most interest to you.

Thanks for your interest in this book. Have fun.

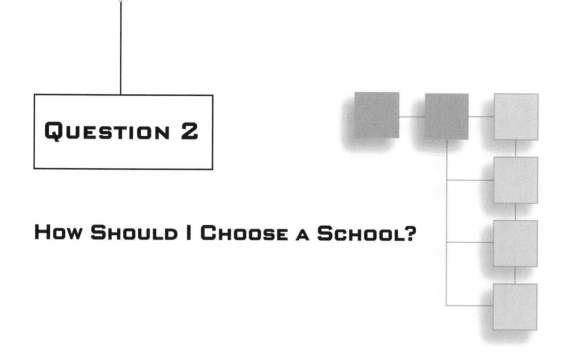

Question 2

How Should I Choose a School?

Ian: Fortunately, when seeking a college education, there are many options. Unfortunately, a lot of these options are wrong for you. Given the high cost (in both money and time) of getting a degree, it's important to know what you're getting. If you take nothing else away from this, do your research!

In general, there are three kinds of degree programs to consider. One is a general, liberal arts degree in a field that's related to games (Computer Science if you want to be a programmer, Digital Art/Animation for an artist, and so on). Then, some schools offer traditional degrees with some kind of game-specific add-ons: game development classes, possibly a game track within the major or even a game development minor. Finally, there are schools that offer a degree that is specific to games: game programming, or game design, or whatnot.

As you get more specific to games, you become less relevant to other industries such as software development or advertising. Although these may hold little interest for you now, it is a concern if you ever decide to leave the game industry (and many do) only to find you are unemployable anywhere else.

Another consideration is the game development discipline that most interests you. Do you want to be a programmer? Artist? Designer? Musician? Producer? If you don't know, consider working on some small hobby projects and getting enough experience to learn which parts of development fascinate you, and which ones are a chore. Or go to a local community college and work on those general

3

education requirements for a year, and get those classes out of the way at a fraction of the price of a private school (just make sure ahead of time that they'll transfer). If you *do* know what you want to do, make sure the program you're signing up for is actually what you're getting—some game programming or game art degrees mistakenly call themselves "game development" or "game design," so look at the course list.

Brenda: There are two questions here, really—should you even choose a school, and if you decide to choose one, what key things do you need to be on the lookout for? I will address the latter question first. When considering a game development program, ask these key questions:

- **Are they actually making games?** What games have come out of this institution and its faculty in the last year?

- **Are they active in the game space?** Is the faculty attending and presenting at game industry or game studies conferences, or are they content to—semester in, semester out—rehash the same old thing? Are the conferences that they're attending actually relevant to what you want to do? Is there just one superstar faculty member who's carrying the load and conferences for the rest of them, or has the institution balanced itself with multiple good faculty members?

- **Does the faculty have industry experience?** Preferably, it's more than just one faculty member with that experience, too. Are they running their own indie studios? There are many programs with a faculty member who made a single game in 1980 or whose view of games is narrowly limited to a subset of games they worked on for a couple years. If you want to get into the game industry, learn from the people who have been there. That said, depending on your ultimate goal, there are multiple programs at the forefront of game studies, too. So, if your aim is to study games and their cultural (or other) relevance, look for faculty who are active and publishing.

- **Does the school have an actual game lab, and are the students making games there?**

- **What percentage of students is getting jobs in the game industry?**

All programs tell you that they are great and give you many reasons to believe why. This is marketing and not fact. Do independent research. The reality is that there are only a small number of good game programs. The rest are happy to capitalize on the growing educational trend.

Now, there is the flip side—should you even bother to get a degree? The game industry does not require a degree like some other fields, so the question is a valuable one. Let's look at why people ask that question in the first place.

- **College is expensive.** It is completely possible—if you have epic discipline—to learn everything you could learn in college on your own. I left college in 1989 and paid off my degree in 2001.

- **College takes time.** College exposes you to a variety of disciplines and knowledge, thus making you a more well-rounded person. Although this seems great at face value, some industry people I know view that time as "wasted" time. In their view, the time spent in Economics could have been better used actually making a game. This is particularly important when indie platforms are rising. The time spent not making games could literally make or break a career.

So, if you decide to brave it without a degree, what will you need to do?

- **You need a portfolio, just like everyone else.** You need to be making games, phenomenal art, or the like. If you're going it on skills alone, those skills as practiced need to be front and center.

- **You need epic discipline.** College forces you through a path, rewards you for good stuff, and penalizes you for subpar performance. On your own, this may not be the case. Many great self-taught individuals were capable of driving themselves toward their goals, however. For instance, while I earned a college degree, John Romero was credited on 29 games.

- **You need industry contacts or others who are as driven as you.**

Alan Kertz (2005, Senior Gameplay Designer, EA/DICE): I have a BS in Computer Information Science with a minor in Economics from TCU. While the degree wasn't a factor in my getting hired (that was more my modding background/portfolio), it has been incredibly relevant to my day-to-day work.

Computer science taught me coding fundamentals, and while ultimately I decided I
didn't like to write code myself, it has been
very useful in my day-to-day interactions with
engineers. As a gameplay designer, it's my job
to design core systems. Knowing how code
works allows me to design simpler, smoother,
and more elegant systems for implementation.
It also helps when interacting with coders as I
developed a keen dislike of edge and special
cases like good engineers. Of course, that also
translates into designs that stick closer to the
KISS (keep it simple, stupid) principle.

The economics courses I took also have been great for design. Modern capitalist-
focused economics all comes down to consumer motivations (on the micro
scale). And Macroeconomics is all about systems. Translating that consumer
behavior focus into player behavior focus and looking at designs from a
motivation angle is extremely useful, especially when designing persistence-
based systems.

Eric Chung (2010, Game and Interaction Designer, Muse Games): Interesting
question you're asking particularly because I'm getting an MFA in Game Design
at Parsons (I'm a student of Colleen Macklin and Nick Fortugno). But as far as
my undergraduate experience benefitting me in my MFA program and at
my game/level designer at a small indie studio in NYC, I feel that it's been
invaluable.

I majored in creative writing and had a minor in marketing/advertising. My
studies have become important precedents and inspirations to the projects
I'm working on. I've taken classes in psychology, philosophy, science, and
math. Some examples of the things I constantly look back at are William
Faulkner, Aristotle's Poetics, mathematical models for optimization, as well
as operant conditioning and the brain's biochemical physiology. When I was
studying these things, I kept asking myself "how the hell will I put all this
junk together and even use them?" To my surprise, I think about them all the
time.

My liberal arts degree has been certainly useful in the academic portion of my MFA work—papers, analysis, presentation—but college was an arena to develop other skills like leadership/team management and being a team player. I argue that amazing games are near impossible to make on your own. Four years of college, being in this club, leading that organization, combines the right setting and age to develop those soft skill sets. Working professionally in teams, nothing is really surprising as far as "dealing with people." I can hit the ground running.

Also, working at a startup, I oftentimes need to take on many different roles. Not only does my project manager want me to design the game, our boss also likes me to proofread things like our PlayStation/XBLA developer applications as well as help with the other team's narrative writing (an MMO we're working on). I sometimes do worry that I'm a jack-of-all-trades but a master of none. However, I take comfort that I'm still on track to my MFA and I haven't been fired yet. I guess that means something.

So I'd like to end my terrible rant with saying, a liberal arts degree is pretty damn useful even if I had to do a bit more to refocus and specialize in game design.

Jake Birkett (2005, Owner, Grey Alien Games): I got my first computer (Spectrum 48K) at the age of 8 (I'm 35 now), and in those days they came with programming manuals. So I learned to program straight away and kept going throughout my childhood on the C64 and Amiga (and a few other computers that friends had)—it was my main hobby, so I put in many thousands of hours. I've spoken to a lot of other 30-something programmers who had almost the exact same self-taught beginning.

I was an academic kid and did well in exams, but by the time I hit 18, I was having too much fun getting wasted and hanging out with girls to care about doing well in my final exams and going to University. I told my mother I didn't want a job—I just wanted to play guitar and program my computer. So she kicked me out of home, and I claimed unemployment benefit whilst I partied and programmed for about 18 months (this was a really intense period of improving my assembly coding on the Amiga, perhaps the equivalent of going to University).

Then I got fed up of having no money and got a job in a computer shop, where I built PCs (and first played *DOOM* on a 486) and learned about Windows. I did that until I was 21 (1996), and then I got a job making business software, which I did successfully for nine years, before I finally quit and began making games as an indie (almost six years ago). I still make games today and I love it! It's sad to think that it took me until I was 29 to follow my dreams of getting into the game industry, but I did learn a hell of a lot making business software. I ended up managing the company, which taught me even more and gave me the confidence to go indie. So in my case, I don't believe that not having a degree is a problem at all, and that's because I was a hardcore hobbyist with a modicum of intelligence. I've met many other programmers (including interview candidates) with no formal training who are fantastic coders, but also some who are not so good, perhaps because their intelligence isn't up to par. Of course, I've also met people who have programmed as hobbyists for years and then pursued a degree, and they are also great coders.

There's one group I've found to be inadequate—people who've never programmed and complete a computer science degree (or a game design course!). By the time they finish, they might know more than the average Joe, but the lack of passionate bedroom coding shows up in many ways.

Jack Nilssen (2010, Founder, Dark Acre Game Development): It seems to me that the business of making games is a lot like the business of writing fiction: the more life experience a participant has, and the better they can communicate their ideas, the better off they'll be. I'm not convinced that school is the best place to get those qualifications.

I attended a year-long game design program at a very famous school. Of the 23 graduates in our class, only two of us are currently working in the game industry, and in both of our cases, the degree we received had absolutely nothing to do with the nature of our employment. I established my own company and started work right away as an independent, while my compatriot accepted a shaky contract deal from one of the instructors for an indie project of his own. And here again that key sentence applies: "Over the course of this first production cycle that I'm putting myself through, I've relied far more on my wits and drive to succeed than on any of the lessons I've ever learned in school."

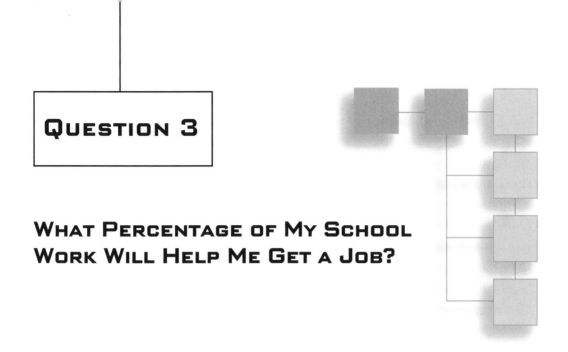

Question 3

What Percentage of My School Work Will Help Me Get a Job?

Ian: There's no way to be scientific here, but for the sake of a number, let's say between 5 and 25 percent, depending on just how many projects you make and the effort you put in. Since this seems shockingly low, you might be wondering if it's even worth bothering getting a degree in the first place (see Question 10).

The other thing you might wonder is, if just going through the motions of earning a degree has such a small effect, what do I have to do to get the rest of the way there? Most importantly, you should be making games, and not just in class. The more games you make, the more you learn about making them, and the more experience you get with the process. More to the point, the industry looks for people who are passionate about making games, and can you really claim to be passionate if you aren't *driven* to do this in your spare time? If making games as a hobby feels more like work than fun to you, that should be a huge warning to you—expect that it will feel the same way when you get a job. The time to consider a career change is while you're still in school; the earlier the better!

The other major component of getting a job is the social aspect. Meet developers (see the entire section on networking in this book). Educate yourself about the industry and stay current on topics; read sites like gamasutra.com, insidesocialgames.com, and gamesindustry.biz, so that you don't sound like a total goofball when you meet said developers. Integrate yourself into the developer community and culture so that by the time you're looking for work, you'll appear to be more experienced than you actually are.

There's an old saying that it's not what you know, but who you know. In the game industry, this should be modified: It's what you know *and* who you know. Those are the things that will get you hired, and while your school projects may provide a core foundation for both of these things, it's up to you to go the rest of the way on your own.

Brenda: My opinion differs from Ian's. Zero percent of your school work will get you a job, or 100% of it will. It's how you demonstrate what you learn that counts. For design and art, the only thing that matters is the output. For coders, a CS degree is a good starting point to get you in the door with game industry recruiters. It also matters greatly how well connected the professors are. Some professors are out there in the industry, going to GDC, networking with and gaining respect in the game industry. And remember that all schools will tell you that it matters greatly, that they have the staff, that they are exactly what you are looking for because they need your tuition. Shop for a college with the same discipline you exercise in looking for a potential mate. It will affect the course of your life. The industry recognizes their names, and by extension, you as their student. When I am hiring, I care first and foremost about games released, industry experience, demonstrated skill, and all other things taken into account, school doesn't carry any weight, with rare exception. That said, the ability of a school to give you the demonstrated skill is important unless you're super driven and disciplined and can get the experience and portfolio on your own. I am reminded of an anecdote. Where I live and work, Silicon Valley, some schools have both a loyal local following and staunch opposition. I know of some people who refuse to recruit from certain schools, while others dutifully get in line.

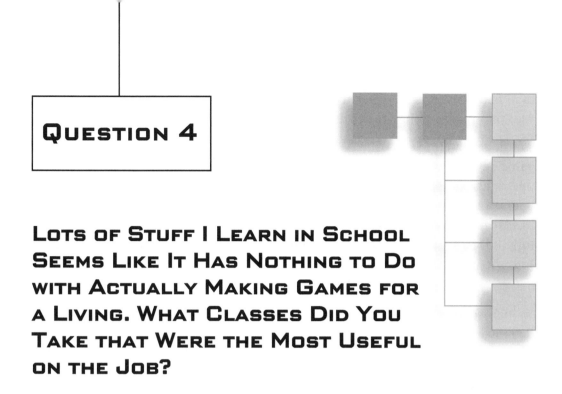

QUESTION 4

LOTS OF STUFF I LEARN IN SCHOOL SEEMS LIKE IT HAS NOTHING TO DO WITH ACTUALLY MAKING GAMES FOR A LIVING. WHAT CLASSES DID YOU TAKE THAT WERE THE MOST USEFUL ON THE JOB?

Ian: In other words, you want to know what you should pay attention to, and which classes you can safely ignore or sleep through. If you are just taking classes to get a piece of paper, or if you are the kind of person who tries to do just the bare minimum to get by, you will probably not enjoy working in the game industry. It's an industry where you are expected to be passionate and go above and beyond the minimum on a regular basis, so this would be a good time to consider a career change.

But that's not what you want to hear. You want to know, with so many subjects competing for your attention, where do you put the effort so that your time is used the most effectively?

First, whatever your major is, concentrate on the core classes that form the major requirements (art classes for artists, computer science classes for programmers, and so on). This is your primary competency, so you want to be competent. That much is obvious.

Second, pay attention to the classes that are relevant to other fields of game development. If you're a programmer, take art and design and audio and production classes if you can find them, for example. This gives you an appreciation for the work that your teammates do, lets you speak and be understood even across departmental lines, and lets you do your own job in a way that makes things easier and more efficient for the rest of your team.

Third, pay attention to your electives that seem like they have nothing to do with game development. Sometimes they are shockingly relevant if you just look at it the right way; a class in World History might seem useless until you find yourself working on a historically-based game, for example, at which point that history class suddenly becomes the thing that gets you hired. The more random little tidbits there are about you, the better your chances of accidentally falling into the perfect position.

There are two other reasons to pay attention to your elective classes. First, the technology in games moves so fast that no matter what you do, you're going to have to learn new tools and techniques, so you had better have a passion for learning. Taking classes in random subjects that interest you helps build (or maintain) learning skills and passion. Second, as cliché as it sounds, it will make you more "well-rounded" as a human being, and the fact that you have other interests outside of game development will be of interest to employers during the interview (if nothing else, it gives you something to talk about to make you feel a little less nervous).

So, pay attention in everything. For every class, try to find some way to relate it back to games (your professor will probably not do this for you, so making connections is up to you). Take classes you enjoy, and work hard on them because you love them. Work hard in the classes you hate, too, because just being able to get through something you dislike and doing it well is something you'll have to do at work, too.

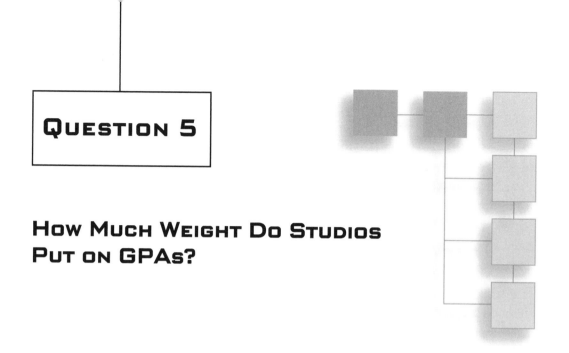

Question 5

How Much Weight Do Studios Put on GPAs?

Brenda: Above anything else, employers place weight on a student's portfolio and proof of abilities via a coding, art, or design test. Consider a programmer who worked hard day and night coding and released multiple indie titles by the time she reached 21. Next, consider a college student who had a 3.98 GPA but no titles by the same age. Provided the students are equal in technical and social proficiency, odds are that the kid with indie titles is the one who will get the job.

Does that mean GPA stands for nothing? Of course not! A GPA is just a number, but it is also typically a reflection of the student's work and ability to maintain discipline over time. Most employers will view the GPA in conjunction with a spectrum of work and in comparison to other potential candidates. For instance, one of the authors of this book achieved a spectacularly horrific 1.2 her first semester in college, but was already working on her sixth game, not that this mattered to her mother. In the end, she went on to achieve Dean's list, graduation, and her mom's forgiveness.

From behind college lines, however, not once has either author been asked to sort potential candidates in order of GPA. All that mattered to interviewing companies was the quality of the students' work. Although this might seem like a great realization and the perfect justification to fail that English lit course you've been struggling through, don't do it. Failed courses extend your time in college, are a tremendous waste of the financial resources that got you there (whether your own, your parents', or a grant) and may serve as a red flag to potential employers during an interview.

Let's go back to that 1.2 that Brenda wishes Ian had achieved. Brenda's performance in her early college years required her to do some explaining in the early going and even 20+ years later as she applied for a master's program. Heading out of college, students with a low GPA will face the same task. The reality is that it will likely come up during the interview at some point. So, if you have a poor or just an average GPA, prepare to explain it should the questions arise.

While in college, it's important for students to focus a lot of their attention on their portfolio. Ultimately, the portfolio—those games—is the proof that your GPA means something, and as daunting as it may seem, while you are in class studying English, there is a kid out there who is doing nothing but coding, building models, or drawing away the hours. That kid may be 1 in 100, but she's out there.

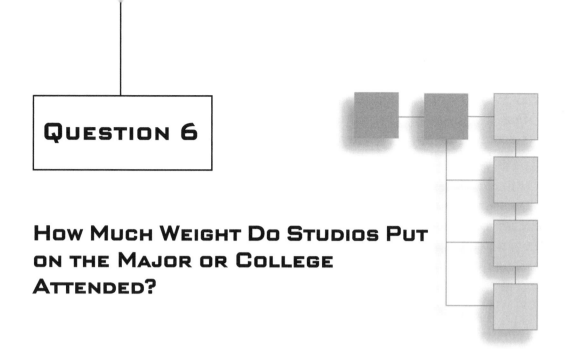

QUESTION 6

HOW MUCH WEIGHT DO STUDIOS PUT ON THE MAJOR OR COLLEGE ATTENDED?

Brenda: Although certain schools are known within the industry—and that matters in certain ways—the rounded answer is, "not a lot." A great school and a great GPA will not save anyone from a poor coding test or a subpar portfolio. A school is only one part of the equation. Great employees come from poor schools, and train wrecks graduate from schools we know and love. Think for a moment. Odds are, you had such a train wreck and a superstar in your own class.

It's true, however, that certain schools have a reputation within the industry for producing some consistently good students year after year. This accolade is the result of good teachers, their own networking within the industry, and a selective admissions process that makes sure that the cream of the crop they graduate were already pretty damn close to cream when they entered the program. You can recognize the programs by their professors—they are involved, making games or contributions that matter, and are known within the game industry.

All major game companies have employees whose job it is to reach out to colleges, establish relationships with key departments (programming, graphic design, digital art, game design, and so on), and in many cases, visit the colleges to interview students. With literally thousands of schools out there, these university relations folk can only visit so many schools in a particular year. So, it's important to realize that choices are being made by companies, and those choices *may* matter to you. When interviewing schools, ask which companies have visited in the last year and further ask about recent student placements. Many schools can trot out a list of students who have been hired by one big firm or another, but that list of ten students may be out of thousands. Ask about recent trends.

As much as these companies are hitting particular schools, they are also posting opportunities on their job sites, so that alone shouldn't be a deciding factor. As far as a major goes, it's a more challenging scenario. Traditional degrees in programming offer truth in advertising. With game degrees, though, the waters get muddier. Some are such a mash of programming, art, and design that the resulting student is likewise a mix of talents, and such a person hasn't developed the level of proficiency necessary for even the lowest level gig in the industry. Think of the degree and the school as two variables in a larger equation that includes practical experience, your social network, your portfolio, the way you present yourself in an interview, and a bit of luck.

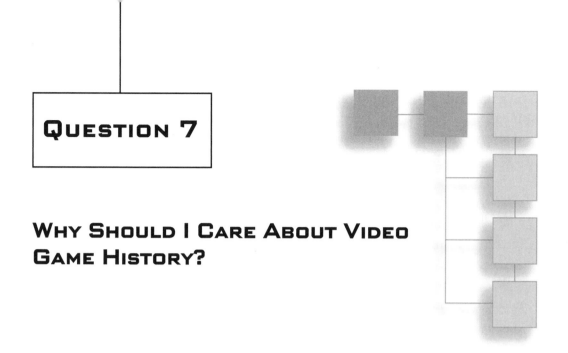

QUESTION 7

WHY SHOULD I CARE ABOUT VIDEO GAME HISTORY?

Brenda: Do you know who Nasir Gebelli, Bill Budge, Gunpei Yokoi, and Dani Berri are? We stand on their shoulders. We are literally living in the time of our very own Mozarts, and the majority of the legends in games are still alive. Some are still making games. They have pioneered a great many genres, mastered programming algorithms and design patterns, and have learned to adapt to platform after platform. When I study a master and his or her games, I always learn something from their process. It surprises me, then, how few aspiring game developers know the history of their own medium and the people within it. I deeply and passionately beg you to learn for yourself.

Ian: Aside from the very good reason that a craftsperson should be informed of their craft as a matter of improving their skill, there is another practical reason to know your history, assuming you are looking to get a job working in the industry: In short, you don't want to look like an idiot.

Not only do games have a rich history, but video games in particular are new enough that many of the foundational people are still alive (and still working on games). What is "history" to you is "experience" to them, and if you aren't familiar with the games that your future boss or CEO worked on (and why they are important), you are simply not going to come across as someone who knows how to do their research, or someone who is particularly passionate about games.

The game industry has a culture, and most people working in the industry are immersed in that culture. Being uninformed about the things that everyone else just knows off the top of their heads makes you look like an outsider or a newbie. Mind you, I'm talking about very basic information here, not obscure trivia. You don't need to have the exact levels of *The Legend of Zelda* committed to memory...but if you don't know who Shigeru Miyamoto is, you will look terribly uninformed.

Conversely, you have the opportunity to distinguish yourself if you make it your business to know the key people, companies, games, and events that have shaped the industry. For example, one year at GDC (2007), I was just idly chatting with someone whom I hadn't met before. I mentioned that this is my third GDC; he said that it's his nineteenth year. I do the math: His first GDC was 1988, and I know that this was GDC's first year... and the only year where it met twice (once in Chris Crawford's living room, then later that year at a hotel), and I asked him which one of the two he attended. He thought for a moment then remembered that yes, in fact, there were two GDCs that year. At this point we both realized we hadn't even introduced ourselves; when we swapped business cards, I immediately recognized his name as one of the foundational designers that I make sure my students study, and I told him as much. Since then, we have both recognized each other on sight, and he knows me by my first name. Had I not been so knowledgeable of his past, he might have written me off as just another random person, and I'd have lost the wonderful opportunity to get to know him.

Henry Lowood (Curator, History of Science and Technology Collections; Film & Media Collections, Stanford University): Studying game history is the best way to come to an understanding of your own place in the industry. Know history to know yourself!

There are several ways this approach to learning about game history can be useful to you. Whether you are a game designer, artist, entrepreneur, lawyer, or anybody else in the industry, game history provides useful lessons about what works and how people and companies have made it work. You can come up with lots of good ideas—game designs, marketing schemes, packaging innovations, and so on—on your own. You might not need a lot of historical study for that. It is more difficult to understand processes for testing and developing these ideas, how success depends on contexts and culture, and how people have worked creatively in different kinds of organizations if you don't have access to historical examples. If you can use history to work out how ideas have been developed or why they failed, you are on the way to a better understanding of your own role in the game industry, how your company works, or how your sector of the industry responds to cultural and market changes. This is an important step to developing a critical sense about which of your own ideas can succeed and how you might make that happen.

Consider two important points about what is needed to make these lessons possible. First, in order to learn from history, you do not need to be a card-carrying historian. It is not necessary to work in the archives or study every trend in the academic literature; if the sources are available, writers and historians will do that work for you. However, and this is the second point, give back to the industry by taking steps when you can to save history for those who will preserve and write it. This might mean securing your design notebooks for an archive, asking a data librarian to help you figure out how to preserve digital assets, or giving a museum permission to collect or exhibit your work. Also, oral histories, detailed interviews, and post-mortems are particularly useful, because they give readers history in the words of the people who made it. Someday, that might be you.

John Sharp (1996, Assistant Professor at Georgia Institute of Technology, Member of Local No. 12, Member of The Leisure Collective): There are many reasons you should care about video game history, but they all really boil down to this: As a developer, it is your responsibility to be informed about your field. This of course means keeping up with the current trends, but it also means knowing the past of your field, where it came from, how it ended up in the state it is today, and how you fit into that bigger picture.

You should understand that the drive to max out technology starts at least as far back as *Spacewar!*

and the Hingham Institute Study Group on Space Warfare; you should know how the first-person point of view developed through a series of id Software games, and how fiercely people debated the importance of the term "computer games" in the 1990s.

The paradox of all this is that if all you do is pay attention to the present, you are only preparing for the past. Conversely, being aware of the history of video games opens your horizons and helps you be part of the future of your field.

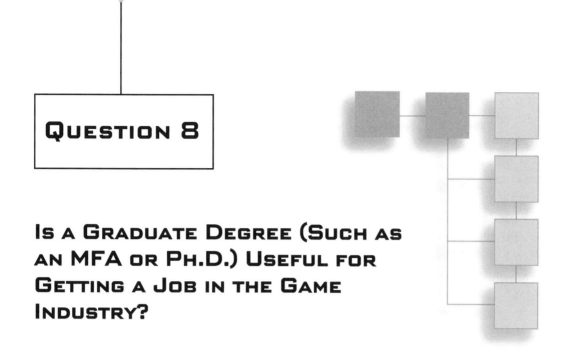

QUESTION 8

IS A GRADUATE DEGREE (SUCH AS AN MFA OR PH.D.) USEFUL FOR GETTING A JOB IN THE GAME INDUSTRY?

Ian: It depends—useful for what?

In grade school, your education is well-rounded, as you take a variety of courses that give a thin foundation in just about everything. As an undergraduate at a liberal-arts university, you grow this foundation with general education courses, and also for the first time, you start specializing in one area (this is your "major"). A Master's degree (such as an MA or MS) makes this specialty deeper. A "terminal degree" (MFA or Ph.D.) brings you right up to the boundary of the field, and earning this degree involves contributing to the field by stretching or advancing it beyond where it was previously. This is a profound experience that leaves one changed for life. In the sense that you will never see the world in quite the same way, graduate degrees are useful for changing how you think. But that is probably not what you wanted to know.

If your career plans involve not just working in the game industry, but eventually entering academia and becoming a university or college-level teacher yourself, a graduate degree is eventually going to become a necessity for you. Most schools are accredited, which is what gives their degree any kind of meaning; accreditation requires, in most cases, that the people teaching all have advanced degrees. Therefore, an awful lot of schools that might otherwise love to hire you will not even let you apply if you're lacking this degree. For this career path it is not only useful, it's critical.

But of course, this is a book about the game industry. Is a graduate degree useful for getting a job working at a game company? The answer, as with most everything: "It depends." The game industry is largely a meritocracy; people do not care about your title or degree nearly as much as your ability to contribute to making a great game. If you find a program that will have you making great games or learning how to make better ones, in the long run this will be useful to you, and I know of plenty of students with advanced degrees who have jobs in the industry. That said, if you are merely going to graduate school as a way of "hiding" from the world because you are afraid your skills aren't good enough ... well, let's just say, be prepared to justify your decision in an interview if you're asked why you went to graduate school instead of making games.

Brenda: See what I said in Question 3 with this one caveat: A graduate degree gives you a controlled opportunity to spend a long period of time on a single project. So does the game industry.

David McDonough (2008, Producer, Firaxis Games): It can be, but it's certainly not a guarantee. An undergraduate degree is usually advisable for any kind of advanced field, including game development. A graduate degree is a much more specific course of study, and in many cases, may not provide more value toward making yourself ready to join the professional industry. But it can provide you a great deal, if you get into it for the right reasons.

Graduate programs are intense, accelerated, and highly tailored to the individual student. They usually focus on preparing the student for more advanced study, research, or teaching in the field at the college level. This kind of study doesn't always overlap with the kind of professional skill training you would want to get noticed by a professional game company. A couple extra years of study in college can mean more time for you to hone those skills or develop yourself toward becoming an attractive potential hire, but those years could also be well spent working up from a lower-level position in a game company, gaining valuable experience and on-the-job training. University programs can only approximate the real industry, and in the end, there's no substitute for active employment to teach you the trade and help you build your professional game development career.

However, a game development professorship can be an attractive alternative to the professional industry. Many game developers have found the academic world to be fertile ground for exploring the art and craft of game development without the industry's commercial focus or pressures. And with the explosion of game departments in colleges around the world, there's an ever-growing demand for new college professors. If you're at all interested in becoming a professor, seeking a graduate degree is vital to opening up that career path.

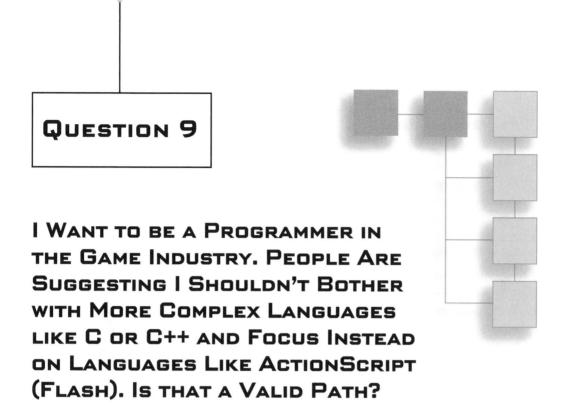

QUESTION 9

I WANT TO BE A PROGRAMMER IN THE GAME INDUSTRY. PEOPLE ARE SUGGESTING I SHOULDN'T BOTHER WITH MORE COMPLEX LANGUAGES LIKE C OR C++ AND FOCUS INSTEAD ON LANGUAGES LIKE ACTIONSCRIPT (FLASH). IS THAT A VALID PATH?

Brenda: Those people are probably not in the traditional game industry. The language of console, handheld, and PC game development is—far and away—C or C++. For graphics programmers working on next gen consoles, it's assembly language. Like it or not, languages are a measure of your acceptance in the industry, and your mastery or dismissal of them will provoke strong opinions from those you hope to work with or for.

That said, a great many coders work in the casual and social space using only ActionScript (Flash) or Java/JavaScript. In recent years, individuals proficient in these languages have been more and more in demand. In some areas like San Francisco, there is frequently a shortage of skilled coders able to program in these languages. So, just going the ActionScript route, provided you are good, can get you a gig.

Ultimately, if you want to continue your career in the game industry, you are limiting yourself to a particular platform, and if history makes anything clear, it's that the game industry is home to a great many platforms that are ever-evolving. Your ability to understand the foundational languages, C and C++, makes you infinitely more marketable and adaptable across a wide range of platforms.

John Romero (1984, Programmer and Game Designer, *Loot Drop*): Hardcore programmers want to know everything about programming, including the lowest level aspects like assembly language. What does C++ turn into? What does the chip execute? Also, not knowing C and C++ is a huge strike against you as these are foundational languages that newer languages are built upon. If you don't understand how bits work or how memory allocation and deallocation work, you are missing a huge chunk of foundational knowledge that will be blindingly apparent to any game industry programmer.

How are ARM chips different from GPUs or DSPs or Intel chips? How do chips pipeline and how do they do branch prediction? These are very low level, complex, but important concepts that hardcore programmers need to know.

Chances are, if you are programming in a language without pointers, you are on the low end of the programmer pay scale. Specialization can change your pay scale dramatically. The difference in pay between a general gameplay programmer and an engine architect is usually $100K or more a year. The more you learn and the more complex the subject, the more you are going to make.

David Gregory (1991, Distinguished Software Engineer, *RockYou*): The one constant in the game (or any) industry is change. The platforms, technology, processes, audience expectations, and game designs are constantly shifting. Players are expecting more and more on a wider variety of platforms. Each platform has its own technical challenges, and sometimes its own programming language.

Your continued marketability as a programmer directly correlates to your ability to adapt to this changing market, and to deliver the best experiences possible on whatever platform is required.

Throughout their history, games have always pushed the hardware and software limitations of every platform. Game programmers are tasked with shoehorning a lot of functionality into every frame. To fit in more features, game programmers must understand the hardware enough to optimize their data and code. The performance of the code you produce directly impacts the features, play experience, and financial success of the game.

ActionScript is but one language of many that you can learn, and that can get you to many platforms. At the moment, it's very good knowledge to have. But the market is already demanding things that ActionScript cannot achieve, and on platforms on which it does not exist or perform well. ActionScript abstracts far enough away from the hardware that there's only so much you can do to optimize it. Eventually, you'll need to learn a "closer to the metal" technology that gives you the power to do what you need to do.

C and C++ provide that access. They do less for you by default. They expose memory directly and allow you to manipulate it as you need to achieve desired performance. They allow you to arrange your data and code to balance the needs of the game and the platform. Knowledge of C and C++ also serves as a great basis for learning and using other languages. Such knowledge makes you ask questions about the cost of other language's features and helps you to decide whether they make sense to use in the context you are trying to use them.

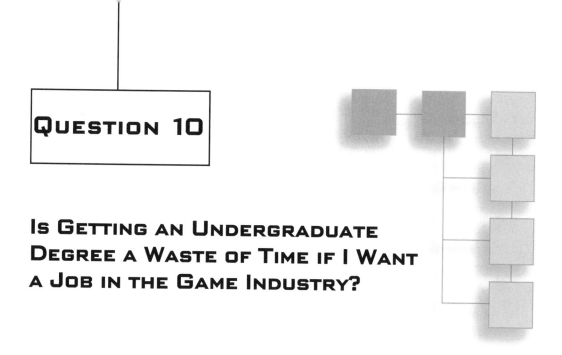

QUESTION 10

IS GETTING AN UNDERGRADUATE DEGREE A WASTE OF TIME IF I WANT A JOB IN THE GAME INDUSTRY?

Ian: You may have heard people (mostly educators) say that you get out of an education what you put in. This is true; if you are merely getting a degree for the sake of having one, planning on doing the minimum work required to get a piece of paper, as far as getting a job in the game industry is concerned, that is mostly a waste of your time (not to mention a colossal amount of money). I've heard it said that there are suitable jobs for people who put in minimum effort: They are called minimum wage jobs. If this is you, you are probably not going to get into the industry whether you have a degree or not. The industry looks for people who will make games, not people who will sit around lazily playing games while other people do the real work.

At the other extreme, if you're the kind of extremely driven, self-motivated learner who is capable of forcing yourself to study, learn, and get hands-on experience without the formal structure of classes, you can probably learn more—faster and cheaper—by doing this on your own and perhaps supplementing with a couple of selected classes for those kinds of things where it helps to have an active mentor. If this is you, a degree isn't a *complete* waste of your time, but you could probably do better without one.

Most people do not fall into either extreme. If you can be self-driven under the right circumstances but also appreciate some structure to your learning, an undergraduate degree (such as a BS or BA) at an accredited school can be worthwhile if you use your time there wisely.

There are a few major benefits to having an undergraduate degree, compared to not having one:

- **You will have to take a lot of classes, and some of them will have absolutely nothing to do with games, at least on the surface.** This is a good thing; it stretches your brain in new directions, something incredibly useful for any developer (especially game designers). This becomes an even greater strength if you actively find ways to apply these classes to games (something that you will have to figure out on your own, as many of your professors will not even mention why their class is important at all).

- **As a credential, it shows that you have met at least some minimum standard of understanding,** which is one step above someone who has no degree and therefore might be great or might be useless (in other words, you guarantee that you aren't at the *absolute bottom* of the curve).

- **Another benefit of the credential is that a typical undergrad degree takes about four years to earn (plus or minus a year)—about as long as a typical AAA (big-budget) game takes to create.** In other words, you've shown that you are capable of starting a four-year project and following it through to completion without leaving in the middle, something that your future employer will expect you to do on their projects.

- **Remember that the game industry has a high burnout rate, so other things being equal, odds are good that even if you get that desired game industry job, you may be looking for work outside the industry after awhile.** If the only thing you can do is make games, this won't be an option. If you have a more general degree, you are marketable to a wider range of jobs, which performs the practical function of providing you money to keep a roof over your head and food on your table. As a bonus, if you find that you have trouble getting work in the game industry, you'll have some "backup" industries that you are qualified for. Especially in tough economic times, it is valuable to find yourself qualified for more jobs than just games, even if the others aren't your first choice.

Brenda: There are a few major cons to having an undergraduate degree, compared to not having one (the compiled *correct* rantings I have heard throughout the years):

- **If you know you want to be a coder more than anything, then code. Code like it is your full-time job.** Start learning *now*, no matter what your age. Many of my famous coder friends either did not go to college or went and dropped out, because they viewed college as a hindrance. While they were taking economics, other people were getting ahead. It held them back.

- **The industry moves fast.** While this book was in production—between the time I gave this talk at GDC in 2008 and the book's completion in 2011—the whole social game industry changed the shape of games. Companies rose and fell. Many 20-year-olds became millionaires. Meanwhile, others got a degree.

- **In my experience as a college prof, every rock star graduate was already a rock star when they came in.** College doesn't make a rock star out of thin air.

- **In Silicon Valley, I have heard it said by people in tremendous positions of power that finishing a degree is a sign that you didn't have a good enough start-up idea.**

- **You'll have a giant student loan.**

- **There are other methods to learn the things you need to learn.**

As an aside, I am not anti-college. I am offering the counterpoint to Ian's point. I am mostly anti-Ian. (I am also kidding. Mostly.)

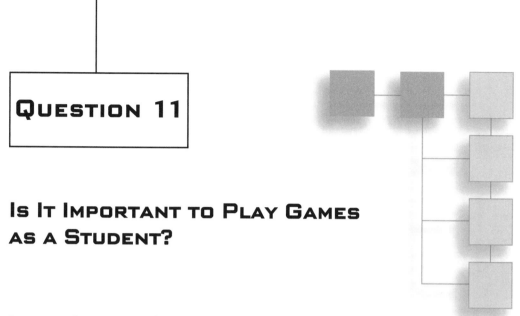

QUESTION 11

IS IT IMPORTANT TO PLAY GAMES AS A STUDENT?

Ian: Yes, but not in the way you're hoping. Just playing for entertainment, especially if you're doing it to escape from the scary task of actually making games, is not going to magically transform you from gamer to game designer.

There are two ways to play games that will improve your development skills, and both come down to improving your critical thinking about games.

First: Play for breadth. Try games in genres that you've never played before. Try the kinds of games that you just know aren't your cup of tea, although lots of other people seem to like them. Play with the goal of discovering why so many people like this game that you personally detest. Play to find the aspects of this genre that could be successfully applied to other genres. I hadn't played *The Sims* until the year 2003 when I was hired at a company that was planning on making a game in that genre. I had to learn to love those games really fast, and it would have made me a stronger candidate if I'd already had such knowledge. I also know a student who had never heard of the "Tower Defense" game genre, and guess what he was asked about on his first job interview? If you're willing to work in only one genre, just as with an actor who has become typecast, your potential pool of jobs will be limited.

Second, play for depth. Within a genre that you like, don't just play to have fun, but play to understand what differentiates games within a genre, what kinds of mechanics work well or poorly and why, and generally what makes a game better or worse. Deconstruct, analyze, and understand the choices made during development of a game as you're playing it.

A game designer playing Shadow of the Colossus (Sony Computer Entertainment) might look at how the climbing, jumping, and gripping mechanics lead to excitement during boss battles. An artist might study the unique art style of the game, and consider how the polygon models for such huge creatures were put together. A programmer might try to figure out how the lighting or motion-blur effects were created through code, or how to get so many polygons on the screen at once.

These examples are assuming that you want to be a game designer, but other disciplines get similar benefits from analyzing games as they play. As an artist, look at the art style. Could you emulate it? How would you go about creating additional assets that would fit into this game? As a programmer, think about how the game was implemented. What are the game objects and systems? What parts do you know how to code, and what parts leave you wondering how they did it?

Brenda: Yes, tons and tons and tons of games. In addition to what Ian has said, I suggest playing games and paying particularly close attention to two aspects—the hook and the grind. The hook is profession-dependent—what are the features you notice first about the art or the tech? What makes this game stand out from the others? What about it makes it fit in with a particular genre? For designers, what is it that draws you back to the game when you're not playing it? These things are gold. What is it that makes you want to play it? I focus on these aspects to help me improve my skill overall. The grind is the core of the game, and is particularly important for game designers. What is the one thing the game is about? What is the repeatable pattern that drives that core forward? Game design patterns present in these games are the tools that you will use again and again (well, unless they're terrible) in your future games.

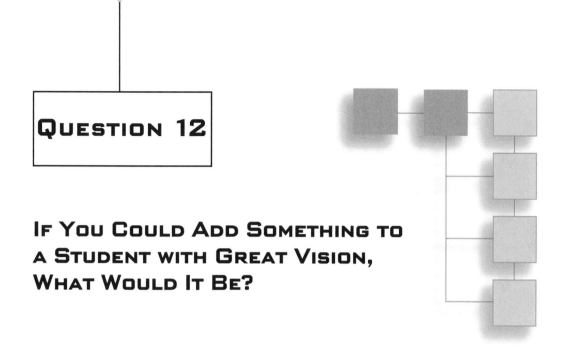

QUESTION 12

IF YOU COULD ADD SOMETHING TO A STUDENT WITH GREAT VISION, WHAT WOULD IT BE?

Brenda: Great follow through. For every 1,000,000 ideas generated by a want-to-be game developer, approximately 0.0001 games actually get made. Often students start a project, dream big, dream even bigger, and then end up not finishing. The single most important ability you can develop as a student and as a professional is execution of your ideas (in both senses). Finish what you start, but kill it if it's no good and start something new. Finished games are what matter.

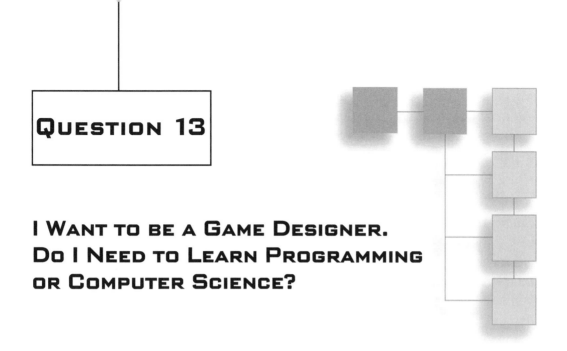

QUESTION 13

I WANT TO BE A GAME DESIGNER. DO I NEED TO LEARN PROGRAMMING OR COMPUTER SCIENCE?

Ian: I've worked with game designers who didn't know how to program. Every single one of them has told me that they wished they knew, or that they should learn some day, because they felt it was a handicap.

More to the point, if you are trying to "break in" to the industry (especially in a competitive field like game design), you want as many points of entry as possible. If all you can do is design games, the only jobs you can apply for are entry-level game design ones (and, if you absolutely must, QA). If you know programming, not only does it make you a stronger designer (and thus more likely to get one of those coveted game design jobs), but it also qualifies you for entry-level programming positions if you're good enough. Having more ways into the industry is always a good thing. This was, in fact, my own path: game programmer first, *then* game designer.

What if you just absolutely, positively can't wrap your head around programming, no matter how much you try? Then maybe you should learn a thing or two about art instead . . .

Brenda: "Need" is a strong word. Some designers, such as level designers, do need to learn how to code in the scripting language required by the engine. Others, such as system designers, can often get by with the ability to work magic in Excel. However, if you're serious about getting the "Holy Grail" job of the game industry, the answer is yes. The reality is that a designer who can code is

39

worth more than a designer who can't. Without code, you will forevermore be at the mercy of those who can, and ultimately, you will feel like an artist who has amazing ideas, but no access to paint, paintbrushes, or canvas. You need coders to realize your game vision, no matter how small it is. Without your design vision in code, your entire "hire me" pitch boils down to an issue of your word versus their hope. "He says he can design, but he's got nothing to show for it."

There are, of course, exceptions to this rule all over the game industry. In many cases, though, these individuals got in early and have accrued substantial experience in that time that makes their coding ability secondary. For others, their creative genius outweighed any need for code. Miyamoto fits this bill. Without coding knowledge, your attempt at getting into the industry as a game designer becomes more and more a gamble. You hope that whomever you're up against is like you—no code experience and no ability to code their own games. Having seen a great many game design résumés, there is no shortage—no shortage at all—of game designers who can code. There's no reason to actively go in hobbled.

What about board game design submissions? Well, sure they might work up to a point, but only if the person reviewing your portfolio is wiling to invest the time. Working on board games in addition to digital stuff shows the breadth and passion of a possible design applicant, but going it alone with board games isn't the best strategy.

Chris Lamb (2005, Game Designer, Powerhead Games): I don't think it's vital for designers to know how to code, but I do think it's important to be able to understand what the code is doing. After many failed attempts at learning some basic coding skills, I've finally come to accept that my raccoon-like brain is too easily distracted by shiny things to come to grips with the complexities of coding. That said, I do pride myself on being able to work with programmers to ensure that, while I may not be able to build them myself, I can at least explain what the many and varied systems making the game work are doing. There are many obvious benefits to designers knowing how to code—being able to prototype your ideas yourself, for instance—but it's not a necessary skill. Work with the people who do know how to ensure you understand what's going on, and don't be afraid to ask questions, no matter how dumb they might seem.

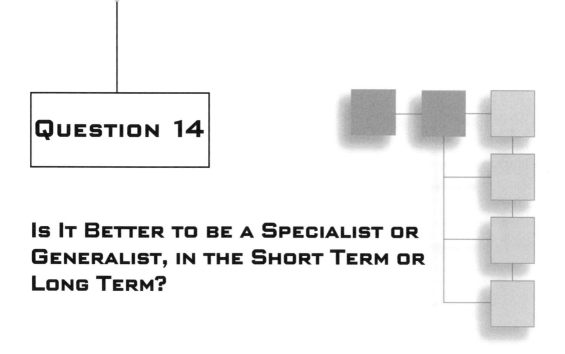

QUESTION 14

IS IT BETTER TO BE A SPECIALIST OR GENERALIST, IN THE SHORT TERM OR LONG TERM?

Ian: Yes. Okay, it's not a yes-or-no question, but there is room for both. It's just a matter of how you want to position yourself and how broad your interests and passions are.

Generalists tend to be in demand in two kinds of teams: very small and very large. Small teams require that everyone "wear a lot of hats." There always seems to be too much work and not enough people to do it. If you can step outside of your "official" job role to get more work done, this is a benefit. In very large teams, by contrast, there tend to be a lot of specialists with strictly defined roles so that no one accidentally does (or undoes) a task that was already being done by someone else. In such an environment, being the person who can speak multiple languages and act as a liaison between specialties and between departments can put you in the position of being the "glue" that holds the team together and keeps things running smoothly.

Specialists have the obvious advantage that they can do one thing really well. Sometimes this can open doors. If you are an expert-level Lua scripter, or localization expert, or you're the best in the biz at network programming, or whatever your specialty happens to be, and a company happens to be looking for someone with that skill, they will find you very quickly.

You might wonder—can you get the best of both worlds by being a generalist in most respects but with one or more specialties? Sure you can . . . but in the long term, realize that you have only a limited amount of time to improve your skills. You will spend that time either building new skills or enhancing existing ones, and it is up to you how to split your time.

Ultimately, then, this is a matter of personal taste. If there's one particular task that you really like doing, and you're really good at it, and you don't need to do anything else, be a specialist. If you have broad interests and prefer a variety of tasks, be a generalist. Either way, find a place where your unique mix of skills is a solid fit.

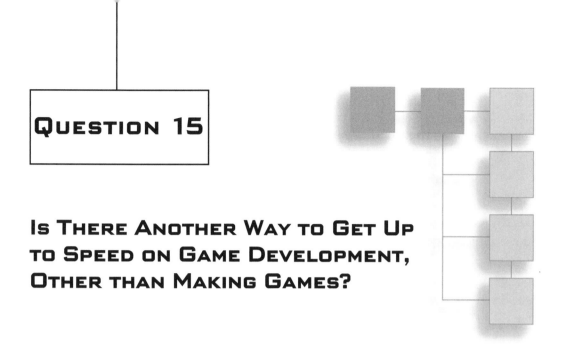

Question 15

Is There Another Way to Get Up to Speed on Game Development, Other than Making Games?

Ian: Does it matter? Suppose there were. Suppose I could tell you that, by reading a certain list of textbooks, or taking a specific set of courses, you could learn everything you needed to know about game development without ever having to make a game.

Then it should occur to you that, having successfully avoided having to go through the (apparently awful) task of actually making a game, you are now qualified to go through this same task as your full-time profession. Did you really win anything here?

Most of the people who are looking for alternate ways of learning are doing it because they either don't find the task of making games to be inherently fun on its own, or maybe they *would* find it fun but they are scared because they don't know where to start. If you are in the former group, rethink the idea of entering the game industry; if you don't absolutely love making games, so much that you actively work on them on your own for the sheer joy of it, you will probably be miserable if you work in the game industry. Stick to playing them instead.

If you're in the latter group and simply don't know where to begin, start by making something small, using what you already know and adding one thing at a time. If you don't know how to design a game or program a game, for heaven's sake *do not* try to learn both at the same time! If you're learning programming, start with projects that have already been designed—that is, make "clones" of other small games. If you're learning game design, use only the programming skills that you already possess (or if you don't possess any, work with board games and other non-digital games). For just about any subject that you want to learn about, there are many books, and just as many free tutorials on the web. Once you start searching, you'll realize how much information is out there and how easy it is to find.

Lastly, you might be wondering if there is *any* other method of professional development, beyond making games. Game developers tend to do a lot of reading. The quality of game development books varies wildly (so look carefully before buying), but there are a few good books no matter what development specialty interests you. There are conferences (notably GDC, and there may be smaller regional ones in your area that are both closer and cheaper to attend) where developers share their knowledge and experience with one another. There are also websites and magazines targeted toward professional developers (of note are gamasutra.com, *Game Developer Magazine,* and *Develop Magazine,* at least as of the time of this printing). Game developers like to share, so it is just a matter of going to places where they do, and soaking up other peoples' hard-won wisdom.

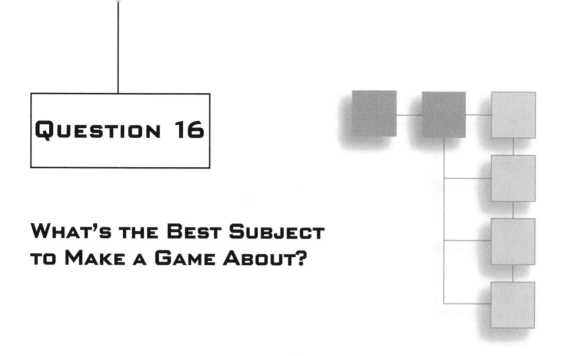

QUESTION 16

WHAT'S THE BEST SUBJECT TO MAKE A GAME ABOUT?

Brenda: Yes. That is the simple answer to every subject you may raise, every single one. The key, however, lies in the game creator's ability to express that subject in a way that does the subject true justice, and in that, there is great challenge. I have made games about material both light and grave, and the more serious topics were my most challenging creations. The important thing is that you make games. Some topics are very overdone, of course. Zombies, pirates, ninjas, werewolves, space marines . . . and do you really believe that your game, which will be compared to the others with the same topic, will be the best? Don't stack your own odds. That said, even among these topics, every once in a while, something new shines through.

The key is to be creative and know your history. In the early 1980s, there was a huge variety of games on all kinds of crazy topics. As the industry became more risk-averse, ideas streamlined themselves into profitable citadels that feel boring. That said, social games, mobile games, and iPad games have brought back that level of topic creativity.

Ian: Judging by the industry's greatest hits of all time, the most popular subjects for games include:

- Italian plumbers who eat hallucinogenic mushrooms
- A creature that looks like a pizza with a slice missing, running through a maze eating dots and avoiding ghosts

- Stacking rectangular blocks as they fall from the sky
- An in-depth simulation of people doing the menial tasks of day-to-day life

If you're looking for a pattern, such as it is, it's that there is no pattern. It's all about the gameplay, not the window dressing.

How do you choose a suitable theme for your game if you want it to stand out? My best advice would be to avoid clichés. There are far too many games out there with pirates, monkeys, ninjas, space marines, aliens, robots, zombies, dragons, and half a dozen other things you can come up with on your own. Also avoid games that are gratuitously vulgar, sexual, or violent; it may give you giggles, but it limits your audience, and will of course be useless in your portfolio if you apply to a company that makes children's games or casual games. In either case, your gameplay will need to be that much more unique to make it stand out as something worth paying attention to.

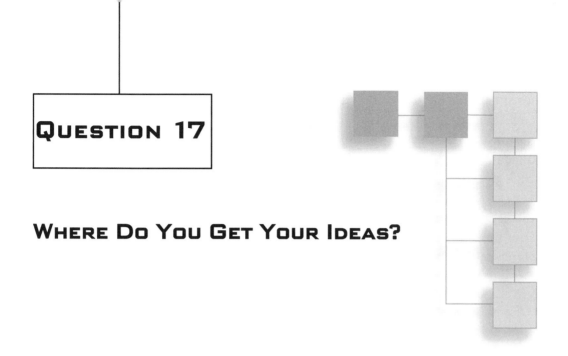

QUESTION 17

WHERE DO YOU GET YOUR IDEAS?

Ian: Everywhere. Game mechanics are all around us. Games are systems, and there are all kinds of interesting systems out there. Just look at politics, the weather, the organizational structure of a Fortune 500 company, the order that airplanes take off and land at an airport, traffic patterns, the placement of aisles in a supermarket ... you name it. Not that a game that is *thematically* about these things would necessarily make a massive hit, mind you, but a lot of these mechanics involve interesting choices and tradeoffs that could be translated into an otherwise unrelated game.

All that said, for the majority of a game designer's career, they do not simply get to propose their own original ideas for games. More often, the source of funding (such as a publisher) dictates what kind of game will be made, so there are constraints. "Design a game with a certain intellectual property (IP) within a certain genre that can be completed by your team in a certain time frame" is common. A lot of times, ideas come out of those constraints; for example, when you work with an IP, you can get a lot of ideas from the source material, especially if there have been other games based on that IP in the past.

Brenda: Like Ian says, games are everywhere. Since I consume a ton of games, I think about things that interest me, and then go about making a game out of that interest in my head. If it's exciting enough, if I want to really play it, it often becomes a game I'll propose or, since I own my own company, just make. I look for situations that excite me intellectually, places I wish I could live, jobs I wish I could do, or people I wish I could be if only I had the courage or ability to morph into that person/place/thing/time. I think about things that I'd like to build by careful tending and attention. With game designers, I think the challenge isn't so much in getting ideas, but in knowing which ones to say yes to and which ones to show the door. Regarding making your own ideas, if this is important to you, make your own games after work, go indie, or put in your time, get a lot of experience, and start your own company. In any case, you can eventually make your own IP.

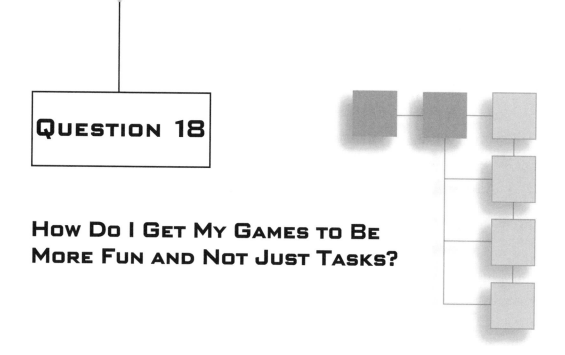

QUESTION 18

HOW DO I GET MY GAMES TO BE MORE FUN AND NOT JUST TASKS?

Ian: This is the heart of the field of game design: taking a game and making it fun. Those who have no training or experience often assume that this is a simple thing to do, as if there were a "fun button" you could press to automatically add some fun into the game. Asking a game designer for some quick tips on how to make a game more fun is like asking a physicist how you can build a simple nuclear reactor in your back yard, or asking a professional baseball player how to swing like a pro. It's not so simple; it takes study and (especially) practice. The best game designers have been making games for decades to get to their current skill level. If there were a shortcut, surely they would have taken it themselves.

Okay, you want some quick tips anyway. Fine.

- **Play-test your game with the kinds of people you expect to play it.**
  Look for any problems that they have and identify the problem points. Make changes and play-test again. Do this a lot.

- **Look at the decisions that the players are making during the game.**
  Do the players even *make* decisions, or does the game mostly play itself? Are the decisions trivial, where there is obviously one right thing to do and no real challenge? Are the decisions meaningless, where they either have no effect on gameplay, or they *do* have an effect but the player has no way to tell what would make one choice better or worse than another?

- **For multiplayer games, do players interact with each other, or is it mostly just each player doing their own thing?**
- **I should probably mention that Brenda and I have written this other book, *Challenges for Game Designers*, which can serve as a reasonable starting point** ...

Brenda: Every game has a core, the one thing that game is about. Every single thing in the game needs to serve that core and make it stronger. If something happens outside the core—let's say the player can do something, but it doesn't affect their core game in any way—they are highly unlikely to do it. Games tend to have repeatable loops that feed into one another. You spend money to become better at X. Getting better allows you to earn more money, which you can then spend to get better at X. For me, studying games the way an auto mechanic studies an engine allows me to see the commonalities in fun games. I also try to make my games simple in pattern thus easy to understand from the player's perspective. I also submit them to my friends for merciless feedback and watch others play so I can understand what people are enjoying and what they have left behind. At all times, I am looking for that nugget of fun, trying things out, taking things out, in search of a fun game. Sometimes, the fun is where you least expect it to be. So, keep an open mind. As with other questions here, an entire book could be written here, just not in this answer.

QUESTION 19

How Do I Make Contacts in the Game Industry?

Ian: The easiest way is to figure out where game developers congregate, and go there. Typical places to look include:

- **Local IGDA chapter meetings.** Go to www.igda.org and see if there's a chapter in your area. Try to figure out where and when they meet; if you can't find the information online, send an email to the local chapter coordinator and ask.

- **Game developer meetups.** Look at websites like meetup.com and see if there are any local informal game development groups, clubs, or organizations.

- **Game-related conferences.** GDC (Game Developers Conference) in California is the big one where you'll see thousands of developers coming together to meet, share, and learn. There are also many specialty conferences that concentrate on a specific area of games, and regional conferences that serve an area outside of California; look around to see if any are in your area.

- **Game-related local events, such as game jams.** Although these do tend to draw mostly students, occasionally some individuals in the industry will show up and participate. They may not announce themselves as such to avoid getting bombarded with student questions (this is called "stealthing"), so you may not even realize who you're sitting next to until you get to talking casually.

- **At school.** If your school has any faculty with game industry experience, guess what? These aren't just teachers, they are industry contacts! They may also bring in other people from industry as guest speakers, and you should make every effort to attend. If your school has a student game development club, they may also reach out to local industry to bring in guest speakers.

- **Online.** There are many professional and casual game development discussion forums. Additionally, many game companies maintain their own forums for their games, so you may be able to "meet" some developers as they discuss the games they are working on.

Once you're at these places, what do you do? With online groups, standard "netiquette" applies: Read any FAQs and welcome messages; read the posts for awhile before posting yourself in order to get a feel for what kinds of discussion are and aren't acceptable, and when you do post, be courteous. When meeting folks in person, the same general concepts apply. Don't be the obnoxious person who has people edging away from you. Don't spend so much time talking that you miss out on the chance to listen to people who know more than you. Do talk to people, once you've learned the kinds of conversation that are normal for the group.

Brenda: Twitter! In addition to what Ian said, get on Twitter and start following game developers. Unlike every other medium, you can just follow them unless they have a locked account (and not a lot do). You can start with us, @bbrathwaite and @ianschreiber. I follow mostly game developers, so look at who I am following, and you'll have a good start. Get yourself set up with a good client (I use TweetDeck, but things change fast), and network away. On any given day, I answer at least a few questions for people. I've also hired interns and employees because of their outreach on Twitter (and the skills they had).

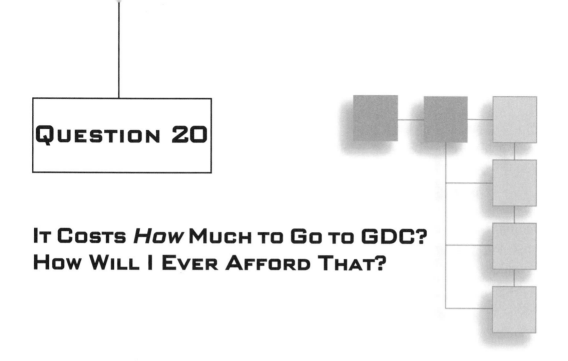

QUESTION 20

IT COSTS *How* MUCH TO GO TO GDC? HOW WILL I EVER AFFORD THAT?

Ian: Students, and even industry veterans, will often look at the price tag for attending the Game Developers Conference and balk. Between a full five-day conference pass, travel, lodging, and meals, it can easily cost $3,000 USD or more. And yet, it is the single largest annual event for game developers, and it holds more career opportunities in a smaller space of time than you can get just about anywhere else. Does this mean game development is only a career for the rich? What is a starving student or game developer to do?

There are actually lots of ways to cut your costs at every step. Hotels are expensive; if you can split the room with one or two friends or colleagues, the cost goes down dramatically. If you have a lot of friends (say, 6 to 10 of you), inquire about renting a suite; you'll get treated like royalty, for less than the per-person cost of an individual hotel room. You can also investigate hostels in the area, which are dramatically less expensive than hotels. Naturally, if you have any friends or family in the area whose place you can crash at, even better.

Travel costs can be reduced by ordering plane tickets early and flying on discount airlines. If you live in driving distance of the conference, you might be able to organize a road trip with friends or take a bus, and save money at the expense of some extra time (if you do this, consider arriving a day early so you're not exhausted as soon as the conference starts). Food costs can be reduced by finding a local grocery or convenience store and preparing your own meals, rather than eating out at restaurants every day; you can also graze on party foods if you find enough parties.

As for the conference pass itself, you don't *need* to buy the full five-day pass. A two-day tutorial or three-day main conference pass is much less expensive. If you buy your pass before a certain deadline, you can get significant "early bird" savings. If you've ever bought a pass in previous years, there's an even deeper "alumni discount" program. If you are an IGDA member, there's an additional discount (in previous years the discount has been more than the cost of membership, making this a no-brainer). And of course, the next time someone asks you what you want for your birthday or the holidays, your answer can be a cash subsidy.

There are also two ways to get a full pass for free (yes, that's right, *free*). First is to become a speaker; this is usually not practical for students or those new in the industry, but if you are doing game-related research, you may be able to propose a poster session that has a good chance of acceptance. Second is to become a Conference Associate (CA); CAs are volunteers that keep the conference running smoothly, performing tasks such as doing headcounts, checking badges, fetching water for speakers, and mostly telling people where the bathrooms are. In exchange for 20 hours of volunteer work, you get a complete run of the place when you're off-duty… *and* you get to meet a lot of great people (including other CAs and speakers) in the process.

Lastly, there are many other game development conferences (including some run by the same company that organizes the main GDC) in a variety of locations, and most of these regional conferences are less expensive to attend. Check your local and regional area to see what's out there. In fact, there are plenty of conferences all over the world to be had for less than $100 at the door.

John Rodenberg (2010, Programmer, Lolapps): During GDC, the networking opportunities and exposure to intelligent conversation about games are unparalleled. The people who speak each year are the best and brightest of our industry, and it is one of the few conferences I plan on attending annually. For me, GDC is about learning new things and finding out what everyone else in the industry is doing. There is also the opportunity to meet up with old friends and new acquaintances to discuss and debate new technologies, design patterns, and the next hot game. During my education, it was one of the best exposures to the industry possible, but it was not easy to get there.

Making the cross-country trip from Orlando to San Francisco for GDC on a student budget was no easy task. Many of my fellow classmates and teachers had already purchased their tickets, but there was no way I could afford the plane ticket on top of room, board, and admission. In order to make the trip more affordable, I applied and was accepted into the GDC volunteer program. Along with working for 20 hours during the week, I was given a full access pass. This made it  possible for me to afford the trip across country. Unfortunately, not everyone I traveled with was accepted into the volunteer program. Those who didn't bought student and expo passes. These passes allowed them to experience the expo and career booths. Despite having a full access ticket paid for, I still attempted to keep room and board costs down. This was accomplished by splitting a room with some friends from school. It was cramped, but we worked it out, and managed to have a good time while doing it. My experience as a GDC Conference Associate was one of the best experiences of my life.

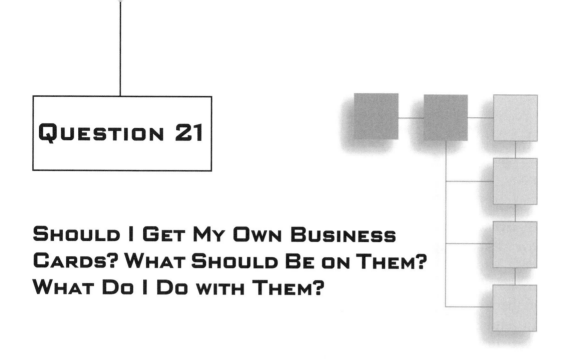

QUESTION 21

SHOULD I GET MY OWN BUSINESS CARDS? WHAT SHOULD BE ON THEM? WHAT DO I DO WITH THEM?

Ian: If you are going to be at any location where you are likely to find game developers, you should have business cards. As of the time of this writing, the cost for a box of 250 ranges from about $5 for a minimal card from an online company like VistaPrint.com that will stamp an advertisement for itself on the back of your card, to $25 to $40 from a printing/copy shop like Kinko's. Places like OvernightPrints.com offer low-cost, high-quality cards (Brenda has used them for years). Cost increases if you print in color, on higher-quality paper, or double-sided. Cost goes *way* up if you print on something other than a standard-size (2″ × 3.5″ in North America) on paper sheets. I've seen cards in all kinds of shapes that had to be die-cut, cards printed on materials like vellum or even solid metal, and cards with a thumb drive attached that contained the person's portfolio... and you can bet those were not cheap. On a typical student (or unemployed developer) budget, standard-size business cards on reasonable-quality paper should not be out of reach, and this is one of the less expensive components of your job search.

A box of 250 cards should get you through your first time at GDC or another major conference, and give you a few left over for random chance encounters, unless you're *extremely* good at networking. So this is a good amount to get if you're first starting out.

Here's what you do with your cards: Give them to game developers when you meet them. This does two things. First and most importantly, they will give you their card in exchange for yours, which gives you a way to contact them later. Second, in the highly unlikely event that you just happen to impress them to the point that they've never been that impressed with anyone before, they'll have a way to reach you.

As a general rule, always, always, *always* keep a few of your cards on you, maybe five or so at minimum, whenever you leave home (most wallets and pocketbooks have a space where they'll fit nicely). You never know when you'll happen to meet someone, whether it be on a plane, at a surprise guest lecture at school, or at the supermarket. In these situations, having a card handy is your golden ticket to getting *their* card, which is something you should very much want to have. Next time you get home, replace any cards you gave away so that you never accidentally run out.

At conferences like GDC, you will burn through cards very quickly, so you'll want to keep more than just a few with you. I like to take a backpack with me so I've got my entire supply of cards right there, and then I'll keep a ready supply of cards stashed in the plastic conference badge holder that they always like to make you hang around your neck. When I notice my badge holder is running low and I've got a spare moment, I'll restock from my backpack. I'll also dedicate some other place on my body to store cards that I receive, so that I don't accidentally give away *someone else's* card in place of my own!

As for what should be on the card, developer Darius Kazemi (2005, Programmer and Evangelist, Bocoup) gives the following advice from his blog, reprinted here with permission (full post at http://tinysubversions.com/2005/10/effective-networking-make-yourself-memorable/).

Darius Kazemi: The business card is the personal currency of any industry. If you show up at an industry event and you don't have a business card, you might as well be playing football without your helmet. Preparing food without your knife. Metaphor making without your imagination. Erm. You get the idea.

In my opinion, your business card needs to convey only a very small amount of information about you. All you need is:

- Name
- Title (if you don't have one, be funny: "starving student" works pretty well)
- Company (if any)
- Contact (email, phone if applicable)
- Physical location (I usually put City, State)
- URL (You *do* have a website, right?)

That's really a pretty tiny amount of information to fit on a single business card. That means you have a lot of room to fit extra material on your card. You may be tempted to fill it with information. In 2004, I decided to make my card extremely information dense, resulting in this little guy:

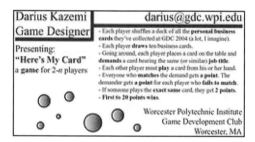

A business card with the rules of a game that can be played entirely with business cards. Certainly memorable, although not as many people as you'd think actually remembered me for it. What *really* worked was my card from the next year, which I debuted at GDC 2005:

The minimalist look of the card is striking relative to most of the business cards you see at GDC, which have gloss and tints that change with the light and embossing and all these other tricks. Although my approach is practically cluttered compared to the web-enabled business card (a card with just your name, implication being they can find you through Google by only your name).

For example, I gave my card to one Xbox developer I met on the first day of the conference. The next day, he came up to me and said, "Darius, thanks to your business card, I'm never going to forget you, ever." I was flattered. Then two days later, I handed my card to a student from Carnegie Mellon who told me, "Hey, I've seen this card. I was talking to a guy from Xbox and he showed it to me as an example of what my card should look like." I'm pretty sure my card was a success.

It's got three major things going for it:

- **The tagline "Producer, Designer, Gadfly."** People remember gadfly, especially the ones who get the reference.

- **The quote "A generally useful guy to know."** By the end of the conference, people I had just met were introducing me to their friends as "a generally useful guy to know."

- **The iconographic portrait.** This is something I subconsciously stole from the guys at Harmonix. The portrait (made by artist Doug Chapel, www.dsquared.org) sports my most memorable traits: glasses, beard, and an orange shirt.

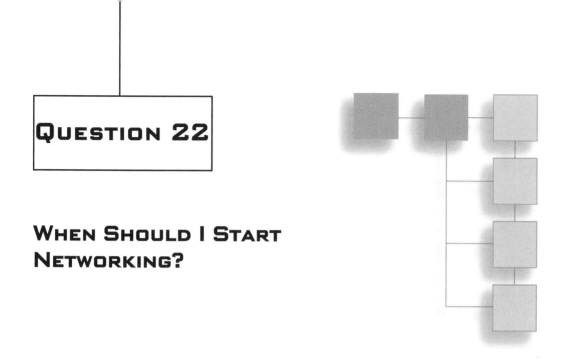

QUESTION 22

WHEN SHOULD I START NETWORKING?

Ian: At birth. Okay, if you're reading this, it's probably too late for that. So, let's say, it starts immediately. There really is no such thing as meeting people too soon. If anything, if you are meeting game developers before you're looking for a job, it takes some of the pressure off them. They know you're not going to be shoving a résumé in their direction, so they can relax a bit.

Brenda: You are doing it already. Just think of a project you worked on or a class you were in. Now, think of that person you'd never ever want to work with again. That is networking. That person has made an impression on you, and that impression will follow them wherever they go. Likewise, think about someone you'd love to work with again. At every turn, you'd consider using them for a particular project. For me, I regularly turn to Ian, because we've worked together for a long time now, and he does great design work fast. There are dozens of others I feel the same way about. Think of yourself—your every action—as a networking opportunity. The person next to you in class may very well be the person recommending you (or keeping you from) your next gig.

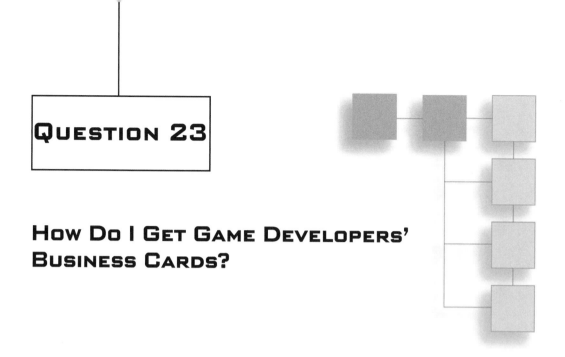

Question 23

How Do I Get Game Developers' Business Cards?

Ian: Take advantage of biology. It's a little-known fact outside the industry that game developers have an inborn, instinctive reflex: If you give them a business card, they will immediately give you one of theirs. (Strictly speaking, the card you give them doesn't even have to be yours, but it probably should be in case they want to contact you.) Naturally, not all developers will return the favor, but you'll be surprised that a great many do.

Yes, this means you need to get your own business cards printed, if you haven't already. Accept this as a necessity. Going to any kind of gathering of game developers without business cards is like going to a LAN party without bringing a computer. Business cards are the virtual economy of conferences, and you will be embarrassed if you have to say, "Oh, I don't have any" or "I forgot them." Get some good ones printed that aren't on flimsy paper. As a word of caution, most large office supply and shipping places will print you cards on the spot. However, they're embarrassingly flimsy. Get your cards ordered a couple weeks out.

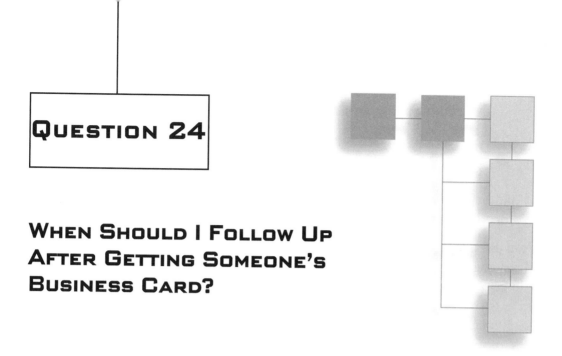

QUESTION 24

WHEN SHOULD I FOLLOW UP AFTER GETTING SOMEONE'S BUSINESS CARD?

Brenda: When you get a game developer's card, odds are you received it at a conference like GDC or another event where developers gather en masse. It seems most logical to follow up immediately, sending an email the second you walk away from them with your iPhone. You're eager to tell them how much you enjoyed the meeting, sharing a couple relevant facts about yourself and maybe even asking a question or two. Don't. Think about it from the developer's perspective. To help you do that, let me tell you about my last GDC.

For the two weeks before GDC, my time was heavily invested preparing for GDC. I was arranging meetings, completing my talks, and figuring out where I was going to meet a particular group of friends to hang out after the main dinner meeting had been completed. While engaged in this routine, the only work that's getting done is stuff that needs to get done. That means there's all kinds of non-critical stuff building up while I work on the GDC-critical stuff. Then comes the giant, but critical, time suck that is GDC. A week disappears in which I am answering even fewer emails while simultaneously generating a ton of things I do need to follow up on. By the time GDC is over, not only am I just generally behind, but I have an abundance of critical things that I need to do. That means that a random email which doesn't strictly require a reply is far less likely to get a response, post conference.

So, when is the best time to follow up? Use Twitter and ping the developer a few days later to remind them of the meeting ("@IanSchreiber Pleasure to meet you at GDC!"). Regular Twitter pings are excellent for establishing familiarity. For longer stuff, wait about two weeks after a major conference and one week after a smaller conference. Follow up on Wednesday or Thursday, though, since Monday is often busy, regardless. Be short and succinct and get to the point. No one likes a wall of text.

Ian: Brenda is correct that the best opportunities to get large quantities of developer business cards are at conferences. However, on the off chance that you did get a business card at a chance meeting, say you were introduced one night by a friend of a friend, or a guest speaker came to your class, or you met at a local casual developer meetup or something, following up that night or the next day is acceptable.

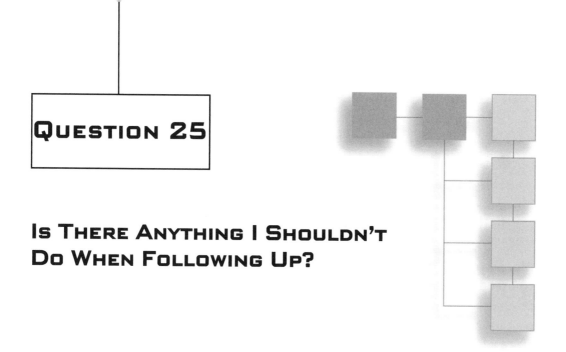

Question 25

Is There Anything I Shouldn't Do When Following Up?

Brenda: Yes:

- **Do not send a wall of text.** When I open emails, they are judged immediately by their length. Long emails take time, and when I am scanning emails, those that can be scanned and responded to quickly have the most luck of getting through. Although this might sound harsh, understand that a typical lead game designer or creative director might receive upwards of 200 emails a day when you take into account personal and professional accounts (based on a survey of my Twitter followers). If you're someone particularly famous like John Romero (designer of *DOOM, Quake,* and the recently released *Ravenwood Fair*), you receive in excess of 300 personal, business, and Facebook communications a day. There's just no way all of that can get answered while still making games, too. In fact, I prefer Twitter over email. It's short and sweet.

- **Do not ask for more than you're going to get.** A lot of time, people follow up with developers asking for jobs, internships, or critiques of their game idea. These requests assume a level of familiarity with a particular developer and set an awkward tone for any future conversation. The email may as well be shortened to, "Hi developer, I'm writing to get stuff from you."

- **Don't launch a reply-festival.** Game devs are typically trying to kill their inbox, getting it as close to "finished" (whatever that means). If you keep excitedly replying to developers, you're going to end up in the deleted bin at some point.

- **Don't assume they actually know you when next you meet.** At typical game development conference, we'll meet hundreds of people, particularly if we're speakers. Reintroduce yourself.

Ian: I would add one general comment to all of this: Remember that any email you send represents you as a professional, so craft it as carefully as you would a résumé or cover letter. Check for spelling/grammar issues. Make it as brief as possible to respect the reader's time. Don't say things that will seem weird or awkward, like offering or asking for deeply personal information. In short, until you reach a certain closeness in a relationship with another human being, keep it professional.

Oh, and even if the business card you received has a phone number on it, don't use it. Remember, this person is trying to get work done, and a phone call is far more distracting than an email or tweet.

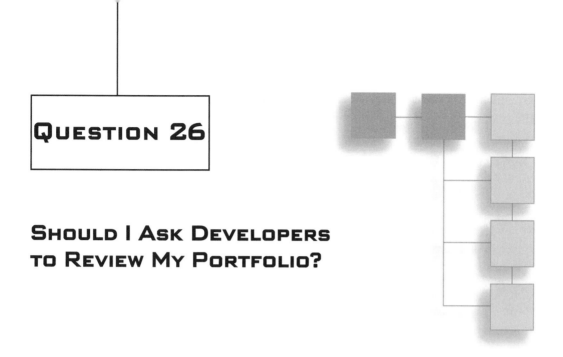

QUESTION 26

SHOULD I ASK DEVELOPERS TO REVIEW MY PORTFOLIO?

Brenda: It depends. It's almost a trick question. If a developer said to you, "Yeah, go ahead and send me a link to it when you get it set up. I'm glad to take a look at it," obviously, you've been given the green light to do so. However, I'd be cautious about using that "green light." You may only have one chance to get your portfolio in front of the eyes of a game developer. Why not make it as great as it can be?

I am often asked to review people's portfolios, and I do because I was once a professor for a couple of years. Sometimes, though, when I hear about students approaching other developers, I often wonder why they'd want them to see anything less than the best they can possibly be. There are lots of communities online and on-ground that are willing to provide you feedback. Join your local IGDA chapter. Participate in any of the art forums out there. These people are some of the most talented and critical people you know, and they provide an ideal opportunity to get realistic feedback. Also, look at other people's portfolio sites, and emulate the sites that you think already kick ass.

So, in short, yes, you should ask developers to review your portfolio if you have been invited to do so, but only after you've made it as good as it can possibly be.

Ian: If you do ask for a portfolio review, realize that you are asking another person (probably someone with a very busy schedule) to volunteer some of their personal time, solely for your benefit, for free. Remember to thank them graciously for their review, even if they are harsh and tactless. In fact, thank them *even more* if they are harsh, as they are doing you the huge favor of pointing out your weaknesses so you can fix them. Someone who just says, "yeah, your portfolio looks good," might be fluffing your ego, but such comments don't actually help you to build a stronger brand for yourself.

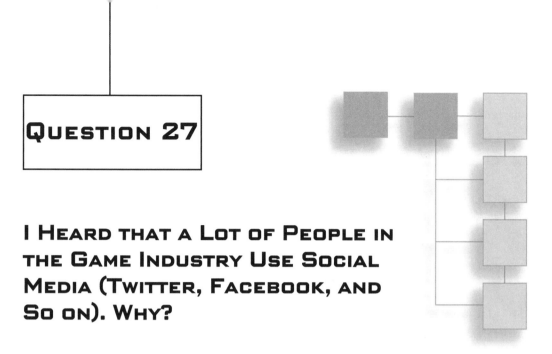

QUESTION 27

I Heard that a Lot of People in the Game Industry Use Social Media (Twitter, Facebook, and So on). Why?

Brenda: In a few words—jobs and community. For those looking to break into the game industry or those already there, using Twitter has so many benefits. You can set up your own account at Twitter.com. Twitter is amazing for finding others who do what you do and developing a virtual community. It's also used by developers when they're looking to find someone for a particular position. In the last few months alone, I have hired five people who responded to a simple 140-character tweet. In fact, there's actually a Twitter hashtag just for that purpose: #gamejobs. You'll find a great many game developers are already on Twitter and will often answer your questions. Get yourself set up with an account and a good program on your desktop and mobile (I use Tweetdeck). Wondering who to follow? Check who other game developers follow. For instance, I am @bbrathwaite and Ian is @IanSchreiber. We both follow a majority of game developers mixed with those who study games. Twitter is also wonderful for getting your news pushed at you. Rather than visiting websites related to the industry, we follow their Twitter feed, and click through if the story appeals to us. All in all, Twitter is a tremendous timesaver; it helps people stay informed and get jobs. Others use it to broadcast new blog posts or other news that interests them.

A social media word of caution: Who you are and what you are in social media is available for everyone everywhere. Prospective employers will go to your Facebook page (or at least your picture). They will review your past tweets.

A few tweets to #gamejobs

Beware the rants, the pictures of you doing something embarrassing, or revealing just a little too much.

Another bonus caution: If you're looking for a job making social games, you should show evidence of having actually played them. Have some posts on your wall and progress through play so that you have an understanding of the space.

Ian: For as much as we live with the stereotype of being antisocial nerds who live in our mom's basement, game developers as a whole are incredibly social when interacting with one another. We like to keep in touch, through email, mailing lists, and more immediate things like Facebook and Twitter. Because of this, over time you will tend to see mass migrations of game developers from one platform to another. First, everyone started creating professional pages on

LinkedIn. Then there was this huge migration to Facebook. Now a lot of information sharing happens (often spontaneously) on Twitter. By the time this book goes to print, it may be something else entirely. Once you have a few game developers whom you are keeping tabs on, if there is some other new social media platform that everyone starts jumping to, take notice.

Harvey Smith (1993, Co-Creative Director, Arkane Studios): In the late 80s, I was working as a SATCOM technician in the USAF, prior to working as a game designer. After going to military tech school and getting close to a few of my classmates, I stayed in touch with them across the planet via teletype. We were all at different bases in Europe and Asia. Working nightshifts, where you could get away with more, I'd send "texts" back and forth with them over these hulking metal teletypes, with  the messages printing out on long rolls of yellow paper. I found that I could stay in touch and maintain friendships even with periodic text communications; somehow, that virtual link kept our real-world emotional connections alive.

Later, in the game industry, our team(s) would often use IRC to communicate all day from office to office, arguing design or pointing to file locations. Eventually, of course, more polished IM clients appeared. At some point, driven by some need to express, constantly updating my website became blogging, and then services like Orkut, Friendster, and MySpace took off. Eventually, Facebook dominated everything else. All this was fascinating. It was at times riveting and enticing; my wife and I met through MySpace. At other times, it was mundane and tedious.

Now I cannot imagine life without these extended connections, which still often lead to video chat, phone calls, and face-to-face reunions. Sometimes it goes south. I've reconnected with people only to have them break with me later because we've diverged politically or culturally. Any way I look at it, communications technology has greatly affected my life over the last 20 years. Enhanced it on the average, I'd say.

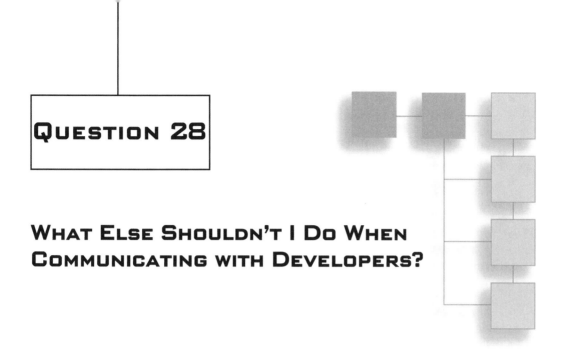

QUESTION 28

WHAT ELSE SHOULDN'T I DO WHEN COMMUNICATING WITH DEVELOPERS?

Brenda: I surveyed game developers on Twitter to ask them what things wannabe devs shouldn't do. Here is a selection of the responses I received:

- @clarkkaren: "Do *not* talk to me about how weird it is that I am a woman who works in video game production."

- @rdansky: "Drop a titanic portfolio on me unasked-for."

- @dhw: "Drunkenly rant at me about how my company didn't answer their application when I'm having an actual business conversation."

- @leighalexander: "Well, I am media, but sometimes I meet startups who want coverage who open their mails by praising my looks."

- @anniemay: "Presume I owe them anything. I'm always open to helping/ being in contact with folk, but self-entitlement irks me to no end."

- @johnneman: "They shouldn't call me. I never use my phone, and it's awkward. Email is perfect, and you're not interrupting."

- @randomnickname: "Don't presume I remember you, or that we're buddies. It sounds cold, but be professional, and jog my memory."

- @laralyn: "Don't send me unsolicited game design documents or art portfolios as attachments or embedded. Make a website and send a link."

- @jenmacl: "They shouldn't send you a new email each day asking why you haven't responded either."

- @danctheduck: "Email me a link to a 20-page semi-coherent rant on their blog filled with excruciating details about the latest hit game. If it is well written, on the other hand, and makes intelligent points, I might read it."

Here are a few of my own:

- Don't monopolize a conversation or randomly hang around too long, particularly if you're drunk. Meeting a famous game developer is one thing. Trying to hang out with them for 20 minutes when they're conversing with another developer they see once a year is just disrespectful.

- If developers are by themselves and obviously engaged in something, don't disturb them, and this includes just surfing the net on their iPhones. By the time developers arrive at a conference, they're probably already a couple days behind on their work. So, their surfing is either a much needed break or purposeful.

- Don't assume they're in the same kind of wild party mood that you are.

- Don't interrupt an obviously important meeting or discussion for a picture you just need to take.

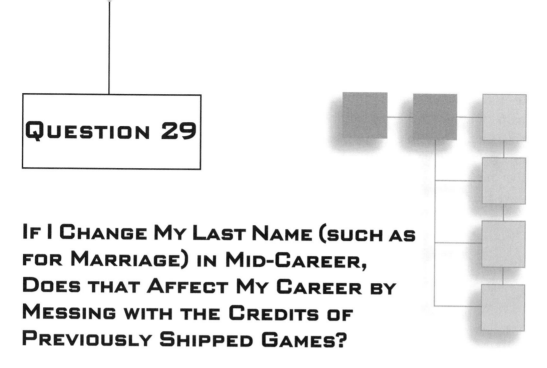

QUESTION 29

IF I CHANGE MY LAST NAME (SUCH AS FOR MARRIAGE) IN MID-CAREER, DOES THAT AFFECT MY CAREER BY MESSING WITH THE CREDITS OF PREVIOUSLY SHIPPED GAMES?

Brenda: Your name is an IP, *your* IP, and it is the most important thing you have. Way before you started reading this book, your name conjures up memories in people who have worked with you, and hopefully those memories are good ones. Right from the beginning of your career, it's important to consider your name and how you will be known. In my own career, my name has changed three times. I started with Brenda Garno, my maiden name. For a couple titles, which were published while I lived and worked in Canada, my name appeared on the credits as Brenda Garneau. Then, when I married in 1998, my name appeared as Brenda Brathwaite. As it happens, that marriage ended in divorce 13 years later. I now have an interesting IP situation on my hands. I am well known professionally by my current last name. For example, my website URL (brendabrathwaite.com), twitter ID (@bbrathwaite), and many professional and speaking credits are all "Brathwaite." This book has "Brathwaite" on the cover. So now, what do I do?

These are the types of questions I had not asked myself or even considered when I married years ago. In fact, I can't find any other people in the industry talking about a name change as an IP issue. If I were to change my name tomorrow and apply for a job, would people recognize Brenda Garno? Do I want to state my divorce front and center on a résumé as Brenda Garno (formerly Brathwaite)? It's less than optimal. Looking at film, one can find similarities of artists who marry and take a name or marry and choose not to. Obviously, it is a personal decision and an important one. For me, I have decided to keep my married last name for the time being. Fortunately, mobygames.com and other sites will list you under multiple names if you marry, divorce, change your gender, or otherwise change your name. In adding this question to the book, I'm hoping that this personal information will be useful to someone, much like it would have been useful to me years ago.

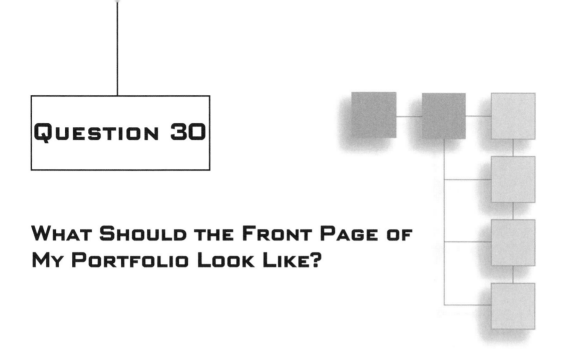

Question 30

What Should the Front Page of My Portfolio Look Like?

Brenda: Every discipline has different portfolio requirements. At its base level, a portfolio is an overview of your skills and work to date. It provides potential employers with an at-a-glance snap shot of your ability, work, level of experience and desired position. It also shows completely obvious things like your name. You'd be surprised at the things people forget.

At a base level, regardless of your desired (or current) position, you want your portfolio site to be *visible*. A startling number of individuals use special plug-ins or Flash on their portfolio pages, turning a landing page into an insurmountable wall for anyone who might visit the site via their mobile device. Typically, this leaves those who hit the wall with a singular question—why? Unless your specialization is with a particular tool or plug-in (a Flash animator, for instance), go with a standard HTML page or at least offer an option for the same. It shows foresight and removes the risk. When it is challenging to get into the industry, why make it more difficult and risk frustrating someone who has dozens of such sites to go through? I know one person who hires artists who flatly refuses to deal with Flash sites. Another recruiter for a major company we all know and love absolutely hates it when artists use non-standard software to play back their reels.

The best portfolios are completely flat in design. That means that your viewer learns a lot about you from the first landing. For artists, this may mean relevant thumbnails all appear on the front page. For programmers or designers, images of games you worked on might be appropriate. The more you nest your accomplishments, the less likely people are to find them.

Your portfolio's front page should contain the following:

- Your name
- Desired job title
- Relevant thumbnails showing sample work
- Contact link
- Links to critical things like your résumé, complete ludography, and so on

Avoid editorializing. No one cares if you want to go to Montana this spring, nor do they care if your girlfriend got a coding job at another game company. What they do care about are your skills, and that should get front and center. A great site to reference, which embodies these principles, is http://carolinedelen.com/.

Your portfolio should be posted online, but it is a wise idea to have a copy of the entire thing on a Flash drive or computer in the event that you run into someone who'd like to see it right now. That may seem unlikely to you, but attend a few game industry conferences, and you'll soon realize that the odds are higher than you think. Trying to get a good wireless signal to show the online version of your portfolio can be challenging, and it would be a pity to miss an opportunity. Be sure to read discipline-specific portfolio questions as well.

Ian: Put yourself in a hiring manager's shoes. You have dozens, maybe hundreds of portfolios to review. What would you want to see? Design your portfolio for that audience, because that is the person who is going to make the decision to give you an interview (or not). Whenever you find yourself slipping back into your own frame of reference ("I want to put this on my site somewhere because I just think it's *so cool!*"), remind yourself that you are not trying to hire yourself, you are trying to get hired. Would that thing you want to add help someone to make an informed decision about whether to hire you? If not, put it on your personal website if you must, but leave it out of your portfolio.

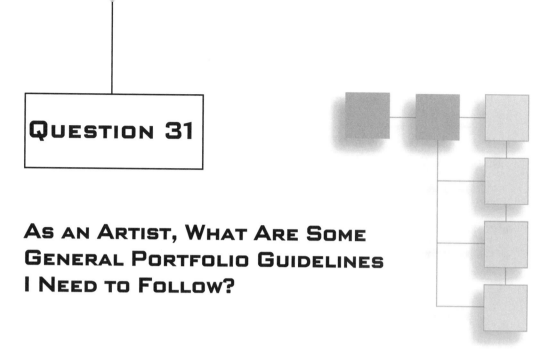

QUESTION 31

AS AN ARTIST, WHAT ARE SOME GENERAL PORTFOLIO GUIDELINES I NEED TO FOLLOW?

Brenda: No matter where you're applying, all artists should follow some key guidelines when submitting portfolios to prospective employers.

- **Show only your best work.** You are only as good as your weakest piece. Many people put in filler material of so-so stuff because they fear that they won't have enough. That weak piece will speak way louder than the good ones. Only show material that knocks you out. If you feel a need to justify or explain anything in your portfolio when you're showing the reel in person, this is the first internal warning that you should remove it.

- **Submit work that suits the studio.** Do not submit 2D social game art to a company that makes first person shooters in polygon-filled engines.

- **Show drawings and paintings if they are good and you have them to show.** Artist and industry veteran Greg Foertsch noted, "All must show drawing and or painting. Maybe I am old school on this, but it is must-have requirement to be an artist. The computer is simply a medium or just a different extension of your hand, like a brush or a pencil. Fundamental art skills are important for all of these."

- **Show assets based on and placed in current-generation game engines.** Nothing says, "I'm not ready" like five-year-old technology.

- **Show separate renders with a separate normal map, texture map, and wire mesh.**

- **If you show cars or motorcycles in your reel, make them creative expressions, not duplicate factory models** (for example, crazed ice cream truck versus Chevy Impala). This is often cited by artists I know as their number one pet peeve in reels shown by students.

- **Note software used for artwork, if applicable, and number of polys.**

- **Open your website with a killer image, not your bio.** Employers don't care where you're from or what you're about (not yet, anyway). That image should speak for you and make them crazy to get your skills.

- **Apply for the job they advertised with the skill set they asked for.** If they ask for lead experience and you don't have it, don't apply. You waste everyone's time, and they may remember you for it.

- **List in detail what your contributions to the piece were as well as the contributions of others.**

- **Proofread your résumé, site, and cover letter.** Have others proofread it as well. When reading these, I often view them as "a $50,000 piece of paper." If you don't take care trying to sell yourself into a job, what are you going to do to my game when you're inside my company?

- **Be selective when including previous experience on your résumé.** Jobs at gas stations aren't necessary to list, unless you painted an amazing mural at said gas station and it's in your portfolio.

- **State your objective.** What role are you seeking? Companies hire for specific jobs, and a vague response to a specific role makes your résumé hard to put through the proper chains.

- **List your skills/abilities.** Employers should be able to tell who and what you are at a glance. Note specific skills in a table or bullet point list so that they are easily identifiable. Don't make people work to see that you have social game or lead experience.

- **Separately, list the software you can use.**

We've included two great articles in this book which address exactly this question: David Silverman's "Building the Ultimate Portfolio" and Jon Jones' classic, "Your Portfolio Repels Jobs." Read both and take notes.

David Silverman (1992, Director of Art, WB Games):

Building the Ultimate Portfolio You're looking to get hired by a video game developer as an artist. There are several companies looking to bring a few good artists onto their staff at any given time. They are taking a major risk when looking for new employees and treat the process like an investment. You need to understand how to make potential employers feel safe in choosing you over your competition.

Employers Are "Risk Averse" In the most general sense, employers look for a safe investment. Hiring people is a huge risk and requires lots of cost and hassle to offset that risk. Obviously it then stands to reason that a potential employer will want to get the best possible employee for the money. The best possible person (at least for production artists) is the person who:

- Can do the job on time, at the proper quality level, without issue or complaint (even the thankless and/or difficult jobs)

- Works well with others (despite adversity)

- Can operate in a self-directed capacity (but always respects and follows direction from managers)

There are plenty of people out there with excellent experience, talent, and skills, but there are far more people on the market with little to offer (despite appearances). Sometimes it's difficult for an employer to determine who the right person is. Résumés and portfolios can both be fairly misleading, and figuring out the real deal can be a very difficult task.

The Importance of the Portfolio   From the perspective of art, the portfolio is, (without a doubt) the most important gauge as to whether an individual can perform at the necessary capacity. It should clearly demonstrate an artist's creative and technical capabilities.

At a glance, an employer can clearly see if you are even in the ballpark of what they're looking for. People applying without portfolios (or ill-considered portfolios) are simply putting themselves in the position of not getting hired. If you want to be hired, it's in your best interest to build a solid portfolio.

Quality vs. Quantity   There is no magic number of pieces to display in your portfolio, as the expectations vary from company to company and (individual to individual). It's a generally agreed upon notion that you're expected to have a quantity and variety that reflects your experience:

- For those with less experience (0-2yrs) or less appropriate experience (like in a related field but different variety of work), expect to include 7-12 images and/or videos.

- For those with more experience (3+ yrs), expect to have upwards of 20 pieces in your portfolio.

Focus should be placed on things you're best at, and never include stuff that isn't your best. If you include things that aren't your best, you're doing yourself a disservice. Anything you include in your portfolio is going to be compared to the best people applying for that job.

Take a moment to compare your work to the best you can find (before submitting your application to a company). Be brutally honest with yourself and know your limits. Don't be discouraged if you don't qualify for a position at your dream company. Even with an excellent portfolio, it might take sending out several dozen résumés to every known game developer just to get a bite.

Subject Matter and Genre   Companies look for one of two characteristics in their ideal candidates:

- Generalists who have a wide breadth of skills that cover most of a game's needs.

    or

- Specialists who can handle one aspect of game development very well.

The major disciplines you're likely to see advertised are: UI Design/Art, 3D Modeling, Texturing, Rigging, Animating, or Concepting. If an employer is hiring for a specific role, send them work that is relevant to that role. If they're looking for an animator, do yourself a favor and make sure to send them some animation work. If you neglect to give them what they need, you won't get hired (and you probably won't even be contacted).

The major piece you'll need to demonstrate is an ability to work from reference or concepts. In addition to showcasing your observational ability, it also can weave a subtle picture of your ability to follow direction (which is a major component of working in a dev environment). Ideally, you should display your reference imagery along with your final art. All work done in any professional studio begins with some form of reference. If you haven't worked from reference before, get started.

Feel free to display work in whatever genre you prefer, just make sure the stuff you show is professionally presented and tasteful. It's not professional to send graphically/bloody violent, bigoted, or pornographic work. When you are submitting a portfolio to a potential employer, be aware that you are telling the employer a number of important things with your work. The consistency of your execution, the quality bar you can be counted on to reach, the breadth and depth of your visual vocabulary, and what kinds of things pique your interests. You probably don't want to add any messages to that list that may give them a feeling that you may not be able to work well with others.

Many companies prefer to see that your interests are in line with the kind of work they do, and others don't really care. One thing all companies do care about is that you have the ability to do what they *need*. If you apply to a company that has a catalog of games that are gritty WWII shooters, you can safely bet they don't want to see your portfolio filled with nothing but Kid's Karaoke cartoon-style characters.

To take this point even further, there are a number of artists who attested to the fact that their portfolio submissions were largely ignored until they updated it with art that was custom-made for the company they applied to. People *do* take notice if you demonstrate that you're doing custom work just to gain employment at the company. This should show that you understand the company (and their games) and that you're excited about working there. There are enough examples of this successfully working, that it really couldn't hurt to try this particular piece out.

For subject matter it's often good to show a character model or two, props/terrain objects, a building or two, and maybe a vehicle. If you have a certain area of specialization (that is to say an area you're clearly better at), feel free to skew you efforts in that direction. Bear in mind that the vast majority of people out there want to make characters. You will have the stiffest competition there than anywhere else.

Modeling   It's good to show mostly low-resolution (3,000 polygons or less) game art, but a few high-resolution (5,000 polygons and up) models or scenes for cinematics are good to show as well. Complex organic and inorganic models can demonstrate a clear understanding of composition, proportions, weight, and form/silhouette, while utilizing a minimum of polygons. It's also preferable to demonstrate knowledge of how to properly structure models for animation (both skinned and rigid).

No model is complete without a texture and good UV coordinates. It should show your understanding of the fundamentals of UV unwrapping: breaking up the model into logical regions for painting, minimizing stretching and seams, proper UV packing to ensure minimal wasted texture space, and maintaining pixel densities across the model's surface.

It's a good practice to display your models with rendered wireframes, smooth (without textures), shaded but untextured, and shaded and textured. Don't just show the model; make the render a piece of art and more engaging. Use radiosity lighting or some other method to really bring out the details. The goal is to enhance the forms to make sure you don't obscure your hard work with crappy texturing, flat lighting, or bad camera angles.

Another important piece to consider is that as next generation approaches are more regularly utilized in today's titles, you'll need to demonstrate an understanding of them as well. Normal mapping, parallax mapping, and displacement mapping each take your work from high polygon pieces and apply them to their lower poly counterparts (making them appear as higher poly pieces). Keep abreast of the trends and make sure your portfolio reflects this.

Texturing   Your portfolio should demonstrate the ability to paint textures from scratch and reference for applying to models and/or environments.

Environmental textures should show the ability to generate seamlessly tiling images that look good repeated over a large area (and blend in well with focal non-tiling art). Textures should show a mastery of enhancing details and forms within the model and creating new details as necessary, while maintaining a balance between visual clarity and visual interest.

When displaying your textures, it's often ideal to apply them to a model. Each model presented should show a couple angles of the textured version of the model, with the flat textures clearly displayed in the image.

Another issue comes with the latest advances in technology. As the art pipeline for games begins to parallel to that of the movies, a greater emphasis in an ability to work with multitexturing becomes important. Bump-mapping, diffuse mapping, and specular mapping are aspects that need to be addressed by anyone looking to land a job at a company working with next-gen technology. This is a far and away different beast to the standard texturing process, which typically calls for lighting/shading baked into the base textures. Maintaining a handle on using these texturing approaches typically found in broadcast/movie productions certainly helps your chances of being marketable.

Concepting   Concept drawings should demonstrate your ability to capture a likeness and/or mood and should act as a window into your creative ability. Your drawings should show that you have the ability to draw technical/ mechanical, architectural, and perspective in addition to organic. Concepts for use as modeling aids should show the ability to draw rotations and should be done in an orthogonal manner.

Animation   An animation reel should show a mastery over the key fundamentals of animation, and should show an ability to evoke an emotional response in the viewer. Keep it short (30 seconds or less is ideal) and keep it simple. Please keep in mind that animation skills cannot be evaluated with still shots.

User Interface   A portfolio with UI pieces should demonstrate the understanding of the fundamentals of best UI practices, and should demonstrate the ability to create cool (game appropriate) UI elements like dialogs and HUDs. If you have the ability, demonstrate your UI skills through working examples: HTML, Flash, and Winamp Skins are all fine ways to show off your abilities. An important note is that UI actually has aspects involving design, programming, and art. A good example here should demonstrate a solid handle at least on the visual aspects, though demonstrating a keen eye for organization, layout, and functionality doesn't hurt.

Submission Presentation   When you assemble your portfolio, take care to display your work in the best manner possible. A good portfolio is cleanly executed and properly organized. Employers often have to wade through thousands of submissions, so not only is it unlikely you hear back from them but anything you can do to make the process simple will reduce the likelihood of their casually discarding your submission.

You should host your portfolio online on an easily navigated site (along with your résumé and contact info). You don't need to get fancy with a Flash presentation or animated links. Employers just want to get in, look, get out (anything really good will be lingered on). Making your info and work available online simplifies the process for the employer and ultimately can decrease your chances of getting lost in the tide of résumés.

Email is typically the best way to apply for a job. It's easy for the employer to manage and organize, and gives them a chance to quickly see your work. I highly recommend you include a good cover letter with URL links to art examples and your résumé on your website. *Don't ever* attach art examples to your email (unless the company requests them)! Including a résumé in MSWord, ASCII, or RTF format in an email is usually fine. Put the position you are applying for in the subject of the email, and be courteous.

Images should be in .jpg format, and animations in a demo reel should be in .mpg, .avi, or QuickTime format. Don't optimize or compress your work so much that it can't be evaluated, and don't make your files so big that it discourages downloads. A safe resolution for images is around 800×600 and 480×360 for video. Warn people if any pieces are over 5MB in size.

It's very important to include a note with each piece explaining what you did on the piece, the software used to create it, and the specifications the piece was created under (polygon count, texture page size, man hours invested, and so on).

Not every company operates the same. Follow each company's submission guidelines carefully or risk having your submission discarded. Some companies like to get submissions in the mail, and others do not. Mailing out submissions costs you money, and if you apply to a bunch of places, it can cost a bundle. So only make physical submissions when you have to.

It's a sad fact that so many submissions are machine-gunned at developers that only a small fraction of them ever reach an artist at all. Most are scanned for errors or compliance to what the company is looking for by someone in human resources. This means that your submission content and presentation is vital. A poorly assembled presentation (and even one that lacks real impact or eye-candy) can spell death to your submission, so please make sure to follow submission guidelines carefully (and only include your best work).

Although these are a good means to reduce your likelihood of annoying a potential employer (and preventing them from discarding your submission), a major component of getting noticed hasn't been fully discussed.

Creative people have cool ideas. Be creative and consider novel ways of getting noticed. I've heard of an example where a guy sent a beer to a potential employer and offered the rest of the pack if they could sit down together over lunch. As was mentioned earlier, going the extra mile can pay dividends. People notice when you've put in the extra work.

Be cool about it, but don't be annoying. Nobody wants visits out of the blue or even cold phone calls. That's the kind of stuff that makes you look like an amateur. If you want to interact with the person in charge of hiring, do it on their terms. If you try to contact them through email or postal service and they don't get back to you, be sure to check back in every couple of weeks in the same manner, but don't invade their space.

Closing Notes   There are obviously numerous obstacles that stand in your way of getting hired. The guidelines presented here are intended to tip the balance a bit more in your favor. The industry has numerous opportunities and tons of competition. If you look at your portfolio as an investment in yourself and a strategic tool for keeping noticed, you may just land yourself the dream job you've always desired.

Jon Jones (2001, Art Outsourcing Manager, Smartest LLC):
Your Portfolio Repels Jobs   I look at game artists' portfolios on a regular basis. These websites are usually designed so poorly that I close my browser out of disgust.

They're even bad enough to turn away potential employers, regardless of the quality of the artwork. Tragic!

Most artists make mistakes like these, but fortunately, they're very simple to understand and correct. I've come up with a quick and easy way to help artists think about how to improve their chances of employment by building a better website.

The core truth here is this: *Usability is just as important as content.*

A portfolio website should be a simple, effective, uncluttered experience from start to finish that leaves a lasting impression on the visitor. An incredible number of websites fail to do this. And it's always for silly, completely avoidable reasons.

Your website should be focused on one purpose, be easy to use, and offer a clear line of action. The following sections outline the three simple questions you should ask yourself.

What's My Website's Focus?   Your website exists to get you a job. Its only purpose is to showcase your art and present your contact information for potential employers. You should make your art and contact information so fantastically easy to see that someone could find it accidentally. If someone wants to talk to you about a job, don't be hard to find.

Include your name and contact information at the top of every page of your site.

For example, any visitor should understand clearly that you are an environment artist and you intend to get a job as an environment artist. Anything else is confusing. Silly MS Paint drawings, photos from trips you've taken, or a blog about your daily life have nothing to do with that, and should be removed. These things are not added value. A portfolio is not a personality test! That's what an interview is for.

The second common mistake is making a website that's difficult to navigate, which leads to the next question.

Is My Website Easy to Use?   You might be thinking "but I'm an artist, not a web designer!" This is a poor but common excuse for making a bad website. On the other side of the coin, many artists who *are* web designers make their website so flamboyantly artsy that it's practically impossible to use.

The first thing a visitor should see on your website is your art. First impressions are formed in an instant. Attention spans can be shut off in an instant. Your top priority should be to make that first instant be compelling enough to keep the viewers looking and to give them what they're looking for. Don't tease . . . satisfy.

After all, did I go to your website to look at a splash page, or art? The faster I can see your content, the better.

Forget splash pages and news pages or any other starting page that isn't putting art directly in my face.

Your portfolio's highest purpose is to show off your art quickly, easily, and with the minimum of hassle. A good portfolio should be so easy to navigate that someone could view your work accidentally.

Anything that doesn't support that basic goal breaks your focus and should be removed or relocated. Make another website for your personal stuff if you have to, but keep your portfolio clean and relevant. More isn't better.

If it doesn't help show your art faster or sell you as an artist, it shouldn't be there.

Here's a quick list of aggravating features that are common in portfolio websites:

- **No image branding:** Every image on the entire website should have your name, email address, and website URL on it. People save images off of portfolios and forget where they got them. If one of your pieces of art finds its way to a studio, how will they find you? Make each image stand on its own, removed from the context.

- **Vague thumbnails:** A thumbnail exists to offer a relevant preview of a larger image. Yet I see thumbnails of random parts of a model that give me no indication of what I'm about to see. If I'm looking for medieval characters, how does a grainy thumbnail of the bottom of his foot help me find it?

- **Multiple layers:** It's as if bad portfolios follow a common navigation pattern:

    Splash page -> News page -> Portfolio page -> 3D Art -> Characters -> Man with Axe thumbnail -> Man with Axe enlarged

Do you expect me not to hate clicking through seven pages just to see your art? Flatten your site. Put the art in my face and show me the quickest, simplest possible way of navigating. One page full of art is better than multiple layers.

- **Multiple pop-ups:** A splash page shouldn't even exist, much less stay open, when you click on it to enter the website. Neither should a thumbnail opening an image in a new window that I have to manually close. I've been to websites that open as many as *five* windows. That's inconvenient, wasteful, and downright hostile toward visitors. Be a courteous host.

- **Poor navigation:** Every page should offer buttons to go to the next image, to the previous image, and to return to the main page. They don't pop up new windows unless it's for an enlarged image, which should be extremely easy to close to return to the thumbnails. It's convenient, it's considerate, and it's easy to implement. It also encourages them to keep looking forward at more art instead of accidentally closing your site altogether. Keep guiding them along a path.

- **Small images:** Small images convey nothing. Keep it large enough to be easily seen *and* understood. Also keep in mind that the average screen resolution is usually around 1024×768, so make it reasonable from that standpoint. Also, remove as much dead space as possible. Nothing irritates me more than loading an enormous image that you only used ten percent of.

- **Bad lighting:** Why would I hire you if your work is so badly lit for me that I can't even see it?

- **Obscure web plug-ins:** Don't make someone download a plug-in to view your website. This will ruffle some feathers, but I find Flash websites to be obnoxious and unnecessary, and most aren't worth the time to navigate. A lot of people don't even have Flash. Do you want to risk losing a great job opportunity over that? Just keep it as simple as possible, but no simpler.

Hiring managers look through dozens of portfolios every day. All the portfolios they see blend together. It's just a job. You are either on the "Portfolios To

Review" list, or you're not. A poorly designed website makes this poor hiring manager's job a little more annoying. Accordingly, he is less likely to invest the time into looking at your entire portfolio. And he certainly won't read your blog. Is he hiring a Metallica fan or a level designer?

Imagine that your target visitor is a tired, indifferent hiring manager whose only desire is to find the shortest path possible to looking at your art. Nothing else matters. So design your website for him. Give him what he wants. Remove what he doesn't care about. The clearer your message, the better.

For example: "I am Phineas Fogbottom, environment artist. This is my art. Email me at mastapimp420@yahoo.com."

That's all he needs to know. Keep it simple.

Do I Provide a Clear Line of Action?   This is also important. Sadly, good art doesn't sell itself. It's one thing to present art, and it's quite another to funnel them toward offering you a job. First you serve up the art, and then you show them that they should offer you a job, and here's how to contact you. The easier this is, the better.

Here are two huge mistakes people often make along these lines:

- **No stated desired position:** The desired position usually isn't obvious. Most artists feel the need to put all their 2D art, 3D art, animation, illustrations, paintings, and even poetry on their website. That makes it impossible to divine what kind of position you're looking for! Be specific. Companies do not set out to hire generalists, they hire specialists. (Whether or not they ultimately *use* them as specialists is another matter entirely.)

  If they're hiring a character artist, your saying "I do everything!" isn't going to make them think of you for the job. It's easy: Be the guy they're looking for by being specific. If they're looking for a character artist, the more ways you can match the pattern they're looking for, the better. A good place to start is by saying "Hey, I'm a character artist.":)

- **No contact information:** If I like your work, how am I supposed to contact you? Keep it visible at all times and don't make them hunt for it.

If you're concerned about spambots farming your favorite email address to add to spam lists, make a new email address solely for job solicitations and just deal with the spam.

That's all there is to it, really. It's simple enough if you think about it, but that's the problem: *Most people don't.* If you start thinking about it, you're already ahead of the game!

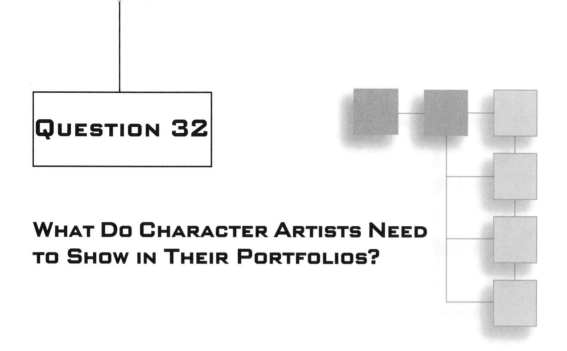

Question 32

What Do Character Artists Need to Show in Their Portfolios?

Brenda: Characters are astoundingly important in video games. It's into that mold that a player places themselves, and it is often the single piece of art that remains entirely visible throughout the whole of the game, stared at—for hours—by the player. The classics we know and love—Mario, Sonic, Link, and Crono—have lived well beyond their original games and are now a part of gaming canon. Even unnamed characters like the space marine in *DOOM* or the millions of player-created characters in *World of Warcraft* are loved by the game's players. So, an artist looking to break in or transition to a role needs to be able to capture that iconic look in his or her portfolio.

Tre Zieman (1995, Senior Artist, Kingisle): Character artists need to know how to make a model that deforms well. It's easy to make something look cool in a static pose, but the good character artist will make it deform convincingly.

Chris Sulzbach (2005, Senior Artist and Lead Character Modeler, Firaxis): The most successful portfolios that I review are the ones that have a solid understanding of how to represent form, proportion, and the relationships between simple shapes that occur in the figure. These three fundamental principles should occur not only in the primary shapes of the figure, but also in the secondary and tertiary details that happen within the character. Something I look at closely, which I don't see a lot of in the industry these days, is a very strong side view of the character. When you look at most side views of models created these days, they are standing perfectly straight with their backs unnaturally vertical. If you look at a person, they have natural curves in their spine that should be replicated in the model. I also like to see a gentle ease in all the joints since your limbs do not naturally stay perfectly straight and locked. Paying attention to these opposing curves in the figure really helps it feel dynamic and alive, and that sort of weight and form adds to the believability of the animation.

Their characters should have strong silhouettes, and they should be presented posed. Any character artist applying for an industry job should have at least the minimal knowledge it takes to rig and pose a model with good lighting and good rendering. I don't care what the applicant uses to render the image, but it should look professional. A good pose will also help tell the story of the character. I want characters with character.

In addition to the posed and rendered character, I like to see model and texture sheets. There should be separate images of both the hi-res and game-res versions of the model from the front, side, and 3/4 view with and without textures applied. There should also be wireframe shots so I can see their topological decisions. I'd also like to see the posed model in wireframe to see how their topology works and also check their rigging knowledge.

I'd like to see UV layouts as well as texture sheets which will show me that they know how to UV intelligently as well as paint textures. I'd also like to see their normal map as well as a specular map and any other maps they use to achieve their final render. Seeing the normal map is very important to me, because it shows me that the artist is considering their final texture resolution in their detailing decisions. Small sub-pixel details turn to noise and compress poorly if the texture resolution isn't there to support all that information.

I'd like to see images of their hi-res sculpts to see their detailing approach. One mistake I see a lot is the overuse of wrinkles in clothes. People tend to sculpt every wrinkle ever imaginable into their sculpts. This looks good in the static sculpt, but a good character artist will take into account the lost and foundness of detail. If the whole model is detailed out to the same level, the model looks noisy and the viewer's eye has nowhere to rest. More importantly, the artist should be aware of how the model will animate. If the artist sculpts a ton of wrinkles into a cape and the cape is rigged with simple physics applied, the cape will deform but the normal mapped wrinkles will not, killing the illusion of cloth in motion. A good character artist will consider the final presentation of their model and not get lost in the details.

In an applicant's portfolio, I would rather see two great models than 10 mediocre models. Quality is definitely better than quantity.

What I look for during the interview:

- There is a lot of ego in character art. Many consider it to be the best job in the games industry, and if you're a character artist, you must be the best artist ever. During an interview, I look for people who have a slight ego, but not a crippling ego. I want my artists to be badasses in their particular discipline, but they should also be versatile. If there is a problem on the environment side, the character team should want to jump in and help out where needed.

- A lot of character art is outsourced these days, so when I am looking to hire a character artist, I want one who will be open to working with outsourcers to get the best and most consistent result. They should be able to communicate criticisms clearly and accept criticism professionally.

- I look for a mutual respect for all disciplines in game development and a willingness to do what it takes and work with whomever to get the job done.

- Passion is definitely important to me, and I want an artist who is passionate about what he/she does, but is also passionate about helping others be the best they can be.

Seth Spaulding (1995, Art Manager, Blizzard Entertainment):

- Show wire frame renders as well as beauty shots.

- Show your UV layouts, spec, normal and diffuse.

- Show good modeling choices—how you worked within constraints making smart poly and texture decisions.

- Do some texture painting and demonstrate the ability to move beyond photo-source textures.

Greg Foertsch (1995, Project Art Director, Firaxis): An absolute must for this position is to maintain a sketchbook. This is my biggest pet peeve among art applicants. If you are going to apply for this job, you have to show that you are a student of the figure. I believe that figure drawing is important to be able to show a clear understanding of weight, gesture, and proportion. Process images (Hi-res and Low-res) are very helpful because they demonstrate process, technique, and topology that will deform correctly. I really like to see the side view of a character model, which is almost always neglected in lieu of the front or back view, because this immediately shows if the applicant understands weight and form. UV layouts and texture sheets are important to see here as well. These texture sheets should show painting skill as well as a good understanding of color theory. It is also helpful to see the concept image for the character, so it is clear that they can translate 2D to 3D.

Tim Appleby (2003, Lead Character Artist, Splash Damage): Good texturing. I see a good deal of artists with a strong grasp of sculpting. I think the development of Zbrush/Mudbox/Crazybump has lead to an outbreak of artists who feel empowered to sculpt, which is great; however, it has also lead to a rise in less of them spending time creating textures. A great texture can save a poor model. However, IMHO that statement is not reversible, and I would rather hire artists with good texturing skills than any other kind. I look for texture detail; however, it's more importantly the approach to the materials, which is key. A good artist's knowledge of color theory will be put to use in their texturing and materials. Complementary colors that appear in specular highlights pop certain details out, while less significant aspects of the model receive more subtle or muted representations of reflection.

When I consider the sculpting side of things, I look for artists who can balance details in their sculpts. The primary and secondary forms need to carry the model while the tertiary details complement it. Over detailing is a common mistake, and I am just as guilty of it. It's indicative of the artist losing sight of the bigger picture, so if, for example, they where painting a landscape, they'd more than likely be focused on painting the blades of grass when they should be still using broad strokes to rough in their scene.

A decent sense of anatomy and convincing fabric sculpting are also very important skills that I look for in a character art portfolio. It's important to establish they have some knowledge of the mechanics of the body. However, it's more important to me that they can sculpt a convincing realization of muscle and fat than know what the tarsals are or where they are located. Fabric sculpting is important because, much like the body, fabrics have to successfully sculpt a representation of one surface resting, pinching, or pulling across another surface.

I also like to see a variety of models. I look for artists who do not want to only make heads! Very often I have seen portfolios nearly completely full of head studies. I interpret that as them having no interest or skill in realizing the other aspects of the character. I want to see enough diversity so that they have anatomy and fabric covered in their portfolio—several examples of fully textured characters with real/semi-real anatomy and fabric detailing. Ideally, at least one of the characters will be created in a photo-realistic manner. It might not be the style of art you are creating for your game; however, a photo-real character is a good measuring stick for comparing one artist's capabilities to others. Stylized work can hide things artists are uncomfortable with and often these limitations are more present in a realistic model.

Finally, I really value artists with technical art skills. If an artist can script in 3D apps or has programming or scripting skills, it greatly elevates them in my hiring preferences. Uv'ing, topology, and character setup/rigging can easily be taught/ learned on the job. Having a good artist who can bring good technical skills to the role (even if they aren't hired as a technical artist) is very useful as they often have the desire to streamline content creation processes they are involved with. Basically, if an artist with scripting skills is experiencing a slow workflow/ process, they are in the best position to write a time-saving script for that job.

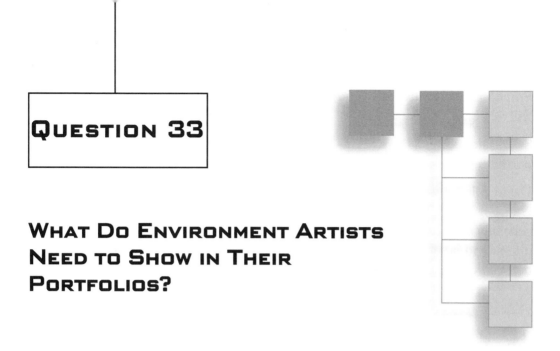

QUESTION 33

WHAT DO ENVIRONMENT ARTISTS NEED TO SHOW IN THEIR PORTFOLIOS?

Brenda: Way back in the 20th century, a game called *Myst* came out. Many in the industry gasped at the game's beauty. The environments were beautiful, even if the gameplay was paper thin by today's standards. You came, you saw, you clicked. In the same year, *DOOM* was released, and its environments echoed the game's ominous, dangerous title. In *DOOM*, the environments were the play. Within those levels, you exerted your mastery . . . or someone else exerted theirs all over you. Environmental artists are a big part of these games. They set the tone for the game within the constraints allowed by the engine. (If you are interested in level design, please also see Question 39.) Nowadays, games like *World of Warcraft* offer huge and varied environments, each of which tells a story. Good environment artists are capable of creating good terrain texture transitions that look natural, good continuity in foliage, and good use of points of interest to help players learn the area. The best way to demonstrate this ability is, of course, to build a game level.

Megan Sawyer Carofano (2003, Environment Artist, Bethesda Softworks): Environment art portfolios should show a variety of scenes. Environment can encompass a lot of things: city streets, fantasy landscapes, or even a small room interior. The devil is in the details, and tiny details like trash, papers, or plants make scenes feel more fleshed out. Overall, quality is more important than quantity—only include your best work, and pieces you are particularly proud of.

Emphasize your strengths and things you really enjoyed creating, and people will be able to see that you are passionate about what you're doing.

Seth Spaulding (1995, Art Manager, Blizzard Entertainment): Build a portfolio of kick ass low-poly trees, and you *will* get a job.

David Silverman (1992, Director of Art, WB Games): Most beginning environment artists generally get a lot of work, modeling and texturing individual objects. It's good to show a range between organic pieces like statuary, and hard-surface modeling for architecture and or vehicles.

It's good to demonstrate the ability to work from photo reference and concept art. Show side-by-side images of a prop you've built with the materials that guided you.

Show off some pieces of fully integrated environments, with the complete scene modeled, textured, and lit.

Demonstrate familiarity with shaders and/or the ability to work with realistic materials. Find a still life or similar set of objects that have a range of surface qualities and reproduce them.

Tre Zieman (1995, Senior Artist, Kingisle): Environment artists need to show that they can create a self-contained diorama of some sort. It's not enough to make a good looking wall or doorway. You need to create a fully realized scene. This is what differentiates between a prop artist and an environment artist, in my opinion.

Greg Foertsch (1995, Project Art Director, Firaxis): The ability to put character into environment objects is important. Show that you can make a trash can with character, and you'll get someone's attention (I actually told a student this once and he went home and did it, and got his foot in the door through an internship). Process images (Hi-res and Low-res) are very helpful, because they demonstrate process and technique. UV layouts and how they handle the unwraps is huge. So, it helps to see texture sheets for objects. It's really important to have some environment renders that show a good understanding of how all the objects in the environment harmonize together through color, value, and lighting. It is also helpful if the scene references a concept image, so it is clear that the artist can translate 2D to 3D.

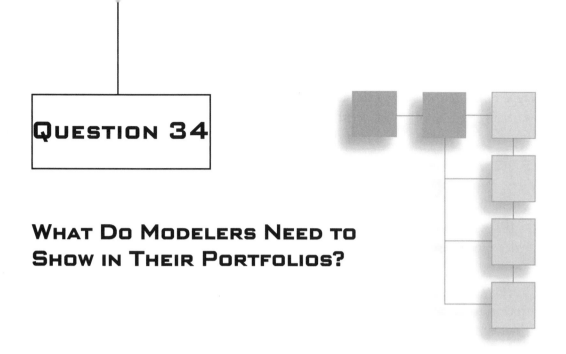

Question 34

What Do Modelers Need to Show in Their Portfolios?

Brenda: Increasingly, modelers and texture artists are one and the same thing, doing both jobs. Be sure to read Question 35 (about texture artists) to take both these aspects into account.

Over the years, one thing I have consistently seen from aspiring developers are models that unknowingly shoot them in the foot. One common mistake is creating models of existing, boring things in the real world. Making a model of a BMW Z4 might be both fun and beautiful, but it's not exciting and it's not game-like. It shows ability to re-create, but not ability to inspire. Likewise, people often create things that are known—zombies, ninjas, and female warriors. In doing so, people fail to see the larger picture from the potential employer's point of view. In a single sitting, he or she has probably sat through 100 such portfolios and seen literally thousands of zombies in their career. If you are going to do a zombie, do you really believe you're going to be the best zombie they've ever seen? Do you believe you'll be the best zombie they've seen that week or even that day? Odds are that you won't be. Another common mistake is creating models that don't at all fit a prospective employer's game style. A realistically proportioned model for a company whose games always include super-hero-like physiques may raise more eyebrows than interest.

Tre Zieman (1995, Senior Artist, Kingisle): Modeling is the fun part that everyone likes doing, but you need to follow through and complete the asset.

Depending on what you're building, you'll need to do UV layout, texturing, skinning, and so on. An artist's reel should never be made up of unfinished models. Of course, it's important to have good modeling skills, but it's even more important to take an asset to completion.

Greg Foertsch (1995, Project Art Director, Firaxis): This is a much more general position and therefore requires a more general portfolio. A good mixture of hard-surface and organic objects demonstrates that the artist has some range. A series of objects that work together (just a few) is always helpful, because it shows the artist can be consistent.

Process images (Hi-res and Low-res) are very helpful because they demonstrate process and technique. UV layouts and how they handle the unwraps is huge, so it helps to see texture sheets for objects. Also, including reference images or concepts shows that the artist can translate 2D to 3D.

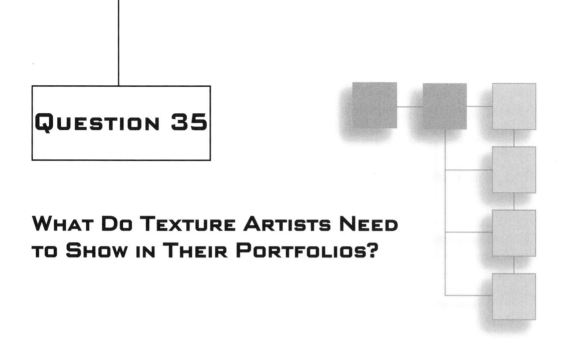

QUESTION 35

WHAT DO TEXTURE ARTISTS NEED TO SHOW IN THEIR PORTFOLIOS?

Brenda: With a texture artist's portfolio, as with many types of artist, a range of styles is critical. Employers like to see both the original textures as well as the end results. Intermediate steps showing the process from beginning to end may also be useful. Samples of the same texture at different scales, textures applied to models, and proof of experience with different kinds of mapping effects are also needed to show your skill. Lastly, prospective employers will want to see your textures on fully rendered and textured models and the very tidy UV unwrap map.

Spencer Boomhower (1993, Freelance Artist, RocketTree LLC): The definition of a texture artist could be expanded to include shaders, and the texture ingredients that go into them. Texture creation has gone from simply putting into a texture what you want to go onto a polygon in the PS1 era, to having to break down the surface of an object into its component texture elements— elements such as the base albedo layer, normal map, specular mask, decals, alpha (for both object edge contours, and edges of decal layers), maybe a sub-surface scattering texture, and different detail levels of the various maps. Taken individually, these texture elements don't look much like the finished surface, but they combine into the very realistic and elaborate surfaces of current-gen games. It's vital that texture artists know how to create and combine these disparate elements and feed them into a shader that represents the final surface, or they may also need to know which texture elements to pass on to another artist, who will plug them in shaders. Again, this shows that artists need to work with other artists in ways that create as few headaches as possible for their teammates.

How to show this in a portfolio? Show the texture elements of a shader, either on your own as 2D images, or applied individually to the model. Like so: http://www.cgfeedback.com/cgfeedback/showthread.php?p=13685. Then show the final combined product. Ideally, texture artists should show work that was created within a team environment.

Of course, if we're talking about portfolios of artists who only aspire to work in simple environments like those found in mobile games, we get back to the basics dating back to the PS1 era: a single texture representing the surface. Maybe an alpha texture if you want to get all crazy with it. These are easily shown as 2D textures, with the final texture shown applied to a model.

Greg Foertsch (1995, Project Art Director, Firaxis): This position seems to be more rare since most companies expect modelers to do this job as well, and most modelers want to texture their own assets. In the event that this is a position that is being filled, it is important to have texture sheets more than anything else. Renders of scenes, objects, or characters should be included. More 2D samples may be expected from this portfolio to demonstrate a clear understanding of painting technique and color theory.

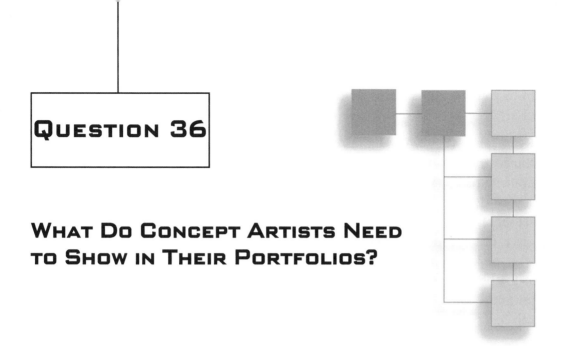

Question 36

What Do Concept Artists Need to Show in Their Portfolios?

Brenda: The concept artist is the Holy Grail of game art jobs. It's what a great many artists and students aspire to become, and it's perhaps one of the most challenging jobs in the industry to get. I could tell you that you can't break in the industry as an artist fresh out of school, except I know a handful—literally five—who have. They were shockingly talented, had been honing their craft long before school, and deserved the position. As a game designer, I rely on a concept artist to better my vision for a game, and to take the game further than I am capable of seeing. Their role is a critical one.

Greg Foertsch (1995, Project Art Director, Firaxis): This portfolio often has a mixture of figure drawing, character concepts, and environment paintings. It is extremely important that this portfolio display an understanding of a difference between pretty pictures and useful concepts. Mood paintings (Mullins) are great for lighting reference and marketing purposes but can be difficult to model from. It is often difficult for young concept artists who are influenced by this type of concept to understand the difference between loose painting and simply being sloppy. Be sure to include images that have call outs and clear descriptions that can be handed to a modeler, especially with mechanical concepts.

Seth Spaulding (1995, Art Manager, Blizzard Entertainment): Show ability to work loosely to generate a wide variety of creative solutions quickly. Demonstrate the ability to tighten up concepts so that modelers can effectively work from your concepts (these do not, and probably should not, be gorgeous works of art).

Ryan Jones (2008, Lead Concept Artist, Telltale Games): There are a couple things that a great portfolio should show. It should show your strengths, draftsmanship, versatility, and your personal voice. The teachers I had in art school always told me you're only as strong as your weakest piece. It's common sense, but it's true. You don't necessarily want to lead in with your strongest piece, but it should be one of the strongest. First impressions are lasting, along with the last impression. You never want to have something with your best piece at the beginning and end and all filler in the middle. It's better to have a small portfolio with a couple of your strongest pieces than a bloated portfolio with sub-par pieces and redundancies.

Draftsmanship is important in that it shows your skill level and also your thought process. It's a good idea to include thumbnails, comp, and a finish to show your process. They want to see how you think and implement your ideas.

Versatility can be key in a studio that takes on many different projects. It's not necessarily a bad thing to be specialized, but when applying to a studio, it helps to show different takes or styles. If you have a portfolio filled with nothing but Vikings and muscle-bound dudes, it might give them the idea that you can only do one thing. It depends on where you're applying, but it's smart to show that you can vary your subject matter and style.

Your voice is also key. There are a lot more concept/character artists out there now. You really don't want to just blend into the sea of all the other artists out there. Showing how you can be unique and bring your own vision into a project can be important. This will also help with the flow of the portfolio. The trick is to include pieces that can hold the person's interest and make them stop and look. Getting something that can draw their attention is crucial to making them want to take their time and look everything over. The worst is to have a portfolio that you think is amazing, only to have the person flip through it quickly.

QUESTION 37

WHAT DO GAME DESIGNERS NEED TO SHOW IN THEIR PORTFOLIOS?

Brenda: Games, games, and more games. Showing completed games in your portfolio is a must whether you're just graduating from a college program, coming in as a self-taught designer, or are a transitioning game industry vet. A game designer who has no games in her portfolio may as well say, "You'll just have to take my word for it," and that never bodes well for future interview possibilities. On many occasions, I have heard budding designers say, "Well, with all my college courses, I just didn't have time to work on games." To a professional, this suggests a genuine lack of passion and insight as well as a naive view of the industry. If you felt so overwhelmed by your college courses, how will you do under the pressure of intense deadlines and game industry scrutiny? You think it gets easier?

When I am hiring entry-level or intern game designers, inevitably, there will be a pile of résumés. Some will contain giant design docs. Others will contain actual running games. I will go for the actual game every single time. It shows you went further, and had that discipline and devotion to see it through. There are a thousand ways for a design to go right and wrong, and the finished game shows me the designer has considered those paths, for better or worse. Completed games or levels will win over a design doc every single time. Who wants to read 200 pages when you can play a simple game?

Although it might seem challenging, select a group of individuals (or go solo) and participate in indie games and game jams. The indie scene is strong and conferences like IndieCade and the Independent Games Festival at GDC offer budding designers a chance at substantial recognition and awards. Even being selected to show at these festivals is prestigious. Game jams, in contrast, are open to everyone and offer a chance to make a game in just a weekend (with spectacular results, both good and bad). Participation shows drive, genuine passion, and might just get you a finished game at the end.

The ability to code in some language is also highly desired. Language preference varies company to company, genre to genre, and platform to platform. For many, the perfect package is a coder who can design games. Many of the industry's greats, from Will Wright to John Romero to Sid Meier, are exactly these types of designers.

Another clue into a person's passion is a "body of work" and play that suggests passion for video games and game design. People who maintain blogs with posts that talk about or dissect video games are useful, provided their analysis is accurate and reasonable. Also, slamming a game publicly isn't looked upon well by people in the industry, in general. Likewise, many developers also do a thorough review of a new prospect's playing habits, as much as they are able to. Facebook and Twitter show plenty of clues to let prospective employers know what a person is and is not into. When an employee applies for a job making social games, for instance, I check out their Facebook page to see what they're playing. If there's no evidence to be seen, it suggests one of two things: They aren't really interested in social games, or they delete all their posts. Neither says good things about a prospective hire.

Steve Meretzky (1981, Vice President of Game Design, Playdom): My stock answer to this question is that the best way to prepare to be a game designer is to be a world-class generalist. Instead of being an expert on one thing or a few things, be somewhat knowledgeable and interested in everything. You never know what themes or subjects your next game will be about, and you never know what little fact or tidbit of life experience will inform your next design decision. But be able to become an expert on a subject quickly, whether it's WW2 era airplanes, Japanese mythology, or models of global warming. And, of course, changing your hairstyle and color several times per day and posting it on your Facebook status is extremely important.

Tom Hall (1987, Game Designer, Loot Drop): If you're looking to get into the industry as a game designer, what practical concrete skill do you have? You may be a writer, lever designer, artist, or programmer. If someone does not have a concrete skill to actually make data, that is worrisome. Everyone has ideas. Everyone plays games. But mere interest isn't enough. Your interest should have driven you to *make* in some fashion.

That leads to second part—an actual game or mod. A work. Something you *finished*. A little 2D game. Something in Garry's mod. Something written with Pygame. Something amazing in *Little Big Planet* or *Minecraft*. Something concrete that shows me you have the passion to make and to finish. By the time I joined Softdisk, I had written 50 games. Finishing games is hard. If you have a game, and just got to where it kind-of-plays and stopped, that's a warning sign. We've all done it. I did it on an early game I tried to make, a copy of *Wizardry* called *Slayquest*. I got the hallway drawing code from *Softline Magazine,* drew up a monster or two, got it to where you had an encounter . . . and stopped. It was so big, and it was too daunting making that big a game from the skills I had at the time. So, I understand. That's a stopping point for most people. Finishing it, tying up every last loose end and detail. Crafting the game. Getting the core mechanic just right. Having an end condition, win or lose. It isn't that hard.

But you should be able to get past that. I did. How? I made smaller games. I made single screen arcade games. I made 15 text adventures. Those were actually pretty good, at least comparable to what was being published at the time. Finishing games made me realize, hey, I could actually do this as a job. And all those games got me my first job at Softdisk, and they published a number of those adventures and arcade games! You can say, ah, times were simpler then, but it's actually easier now! There are great tools and software libraries and games to mod. Just look at all the web games that are out there. 300,000 iPhone games. Mostly simple small games. One or two or three people can still make a wildly popular game. And finishing a reasonably-scoped game doesn't take that long.

For instance, I did a very simple clone of *Galaxian* called *Bugaboo* in *Anachronox*. I did the graphics, sound, code, everything in 15 hours. It was in our scripting language, but there are plenty of scripting languages and tools out there. Or just make it in text! Graphics don't matter. Gameplay does. Finishing does. There's really no excuse not to make a game. You can't code? Find someone who can. Or make a mod. Or be like Brenda and make a non-digital game. Now there are no barriers, no excuses as to why you couldn't finish. Make a new game with a checkerboard. Or with D&D figurines. With a piece of paper and dimes and pennies. You want to make games ... *why aren't you making games*? It's not some magic baton that someone hands you. It's not a conch shell you're given and now you are the authority to start enacting your vision. Your desire should have given you the power, and your persistence should have produced a game.

Thirdly, I look for a creative spark. Many people come in and say how their version of *World of Warcraft* would feature this, or their *Call of Duty* would have a cooler weapon. That's more desire fulfillment than design. It also hubris to assume from making nothing you can go make a AAA title. Sure, that can be a dream, but you have to take the steps to that dream, to work at it. And have a mind for design.

When you interview, I will give you a few scenarios in a game, and ask how the player gets through them. Truly creative people will ask, "how many do you want?" and rattle them off. It's sort of an impromptu definition of a game design. What does the player get to do? What are you teaching them to do at the start of the game? And how pedestrian are your ideas?

Take the well-worn interview scenario, "You are the player, starting our new game, locked in a castle prison cell. How do you get out?" It's so easy to say, "They attract the guard's attention, then grab him through the bars." This is the predictable rom-com of design. "You search and find a key" is, too. Wow, your abductors overlooked that!

What I want to hear is how you are starting your game, and what new thing are you immediately teaching the player. Could be something simple but mechanic- and environment-aware, like:

- "I am a monk. I learn how to hop from wall to wall, reaching a window 40 feet up."

- "My abductors don't know I am a spirit mage. I learn through a few prompts how to take spirit form, and walk through the bars. It takes most of my energy, so I know I must use it sparingly."

- "I am told I will die of starvation in this secret cell and will never get out. However, I am immortal; I learn the time-acceleration mechanic, and stand in place for centuries while the castle crumbles around me. Being able to travel through time in a place where I will not be inter-rupted will give me access to inaccessible areas if I am clever."

Create something novel and understand that these are the first moments of a game, and you are teaching the players critical things. You are defining the experience from the cloud of infinite possibilities. You are telling the players what they can and can't do. You are giving them rules. And you're showing me you can come up with solutions as a designer, creative ways to make things happen given parameters. I'm giving you rules. You are playing the game of game design.

Yes, it would be great if you can make a coherent game design document and have an example. Yes, it would be good if you can break down small games into tasks for programming, art, design, and sound, what I call PADS. But that can be taught. Passion and creativity and persistence cannot. You say you want to make games. Don't tell me. Show me.

Kim McAuliffe (1995, Game Designer, Microsoft Game Studios): Play games—and not just the games in your favorite genre. Play what your mom is playing on Facebook and figure out why it's so compelling to her even if it's not to you. Play things normally out of your comfort zone. Being able to talk about any genre at will is valuable. Play board games, card games, everything. Analyze the major systems as you play, figure out how they work together to form a cohesive experience, decide what you feel works really well and what you think is broken. Know what rubber-banding is. Notice when something feels too random, or not random enough. Modify the rules; create your own.

In every interview I can remember, I've been asked, "If you could make any game, what would you make?" Have an interesting answer ready for that, not just "I really want to work on Sequel X." What would you do that hasn't already been done? Also, do your homework before interviews. Play the company's games and dissect them. Talk about what you like, but more importantly, talk about what you don't like and how you would change things to make the game better.

Be willing to start out as a level designer, and play with level editors to create your own. It might not be possible to leap straight into systems design without prior experience, and on smaller projects/teams, you might be called on to do both. Even if you don't end up in level design, you need to know what level designers do.

Be multifaceted. If you're in school, take classes in writing, art, programming, and public speaking. Being able to organize, explain, and present your creative ideas is as important as generating them. You will be writing documents for an entire development team and/or clients to read, so they have to be clear and concise and use good grammar. Having a basic knowledge of what the artists and programmers who will be implementing your ideas do makes you a valuable commodity to hiring managers.

Stay current with industry news and trends. Add RSS feeds from major game sites to your daily reader; follow industry vets on Twitter to see what they think is hot and noteworthy.

The best tactic is to make a game. Having something playable that demonstrates your creativity, knowledge, and skill says more than an artfully written résumé.

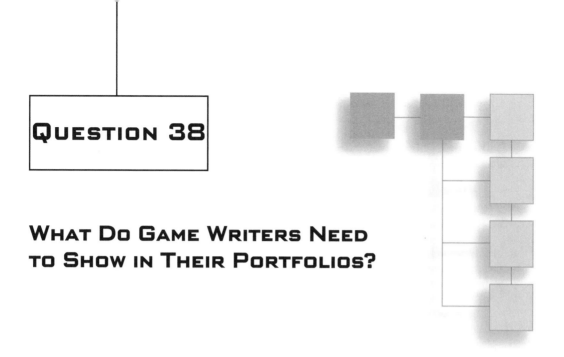

QUESTION 38

WHAT DO GAME WRITERS NEED TO SHOW IN THEIR PORTFOLIOS?

Brenda: The role of the game writer is a varied one. From quests, to NPC dialogue, to game manuals, to complete story lines, game writers may be called upon to do it all. The dialogue and story may be the writer's creation, or she may be following the lead's direction. In my time in the industry, I have done it all. When I am writing for games, first and foremost, I consider the world's lore, and I use every opportunity to expand and deepen the lore of the game. I want the overall IP (intellectual property) space to be rich. I also want people to feel attached to my characters. In writing dialogue for the *Jagged Alliance* characters, I had to write characters from scratch and expand on characters that were created by Shawn Lyng. In both cases, I had to mimic his voice and his direction. For the *Wizardry* series, however, my role was a much larger one. I sometimes wrote manuals and other times wrote dialogue. By the time I got to the end of the series, I was creating the entire world's story, including the level design, character design, NPC design, and PC dialogue to support it. It was a massive undertaking. For aspiring game writers, that goal may be years away. To start, I recommend:

- **Proof your stuff.** I have seen an astonishing number of portfolios with errors. If you want to write, make your letter and résumé perfect.

- **Create sample quests or characters for a game that your prospective employer has published or is working on.** Show me that you can pick

119

up existing IP and move forward with it. Show me you can mimic my style.

- **Publish.** Write about games, some how, some way. My first writing job for games occurred when I was a whopping 21 years old. I said I'd write a manual for *Wizardry 5*, and they actually let me. I have since worked with many interns and junior game designers, giving them a critical credit needed to break in.

- **Network.** The game writers are a very well organized group. The IGDA Writer's SIG offers everything an aspiring game writer needs and holds regular gatherings at game industry conferences, too.

Christy Marx (1988, Senior Game Designer and Narrative Designer, Zynga): First, an impressive list of professional credits helps you more than anything else. They don't have to be game credits. Pretty much any kind of professional writing credit will make the difference in getting a foot in the door.

In terms of writing samples, it's important to show that you know how to think in terms of visual storytelling, that your writing reflects your understanding of the game medium, which is that it tells a story primarily through two senses: what the player sees and what the player hears.

Although it doesn't hurt to include something like a published short story (meaning a valid professional sale), I feel you're better served by using samples that are written in a script format, ideally an animation script format because games use animation. This will show your mastery of a tightly focused form of writing that displays description, action, pacing, and dialogue writing abilities.

It can't hurt to include something along the lines of a game bible in which you show your skill at creating well thought out worlds, character biographies, and backstory.

However, and this is important, you must keep everything *short*. The kinds of people you want to reach are producers or project managers who are insanely busy and don't have a lot of time to spare for reading. So pick what is absolutely your best work, pare it down to something as short as possible without sacrificing the essence of it, and hope it will actually get read.

Richard Dansky (1999, Central Clancy Writer, Red Storm Ubisoft): The simple answer is "whatever proves you can write." The more accurate and appropriate answer is "whatever proves you can write for games." If your portfolio demonstrates that you are a wonderful novelist/comics writer/screenplay writer/composer of haiku/writer of *Star Trek/My Little Pony* crossover fan, that's all  well and good, but it doesn't really get you any closer to convincing someone that you can in fact handle the unique needs and demands of writing for games.

What you really need in your portfolio is a selection of material that showcases two skills. One, that you can in fact string words together in a way that is reasonably competent, and two, that you have thought about what particular patterns those words need to go in so that they might possibly support a player experience in a game. The first part is (relatively) easy, as far as such things go. Hopefully, you're at least reasonably proficient at that whole "writing" thing before you decide to go hunting a job as a game writer. It's the second one that trips people up.

Part of demonstrating that you can write to the demands of a game is the proper format for your portfolio content—or should I say proper formats. Game writing, particularly on larger projects, can take many forms. Sure, there's the big flashy cinematic sequences, but there's also in-game text, systemic dialogue, game artifact text, and more. None of these is as glamorous as the big intro cinematic with lots of dragons, explosions, and exploding dragons, but they're at least as important to the overall game experience. (If you doubt me, I want you to think about the last FPS you played. Think about how much of the game was spent watching cinematics. Then think about how much of the game was spent listening to people yell "Arggh!" and "Medic!" and "He shot me!" Odds are, the scales tilt considerably away from the cut scene in that particular bit of accounting.)

All of which means that if you understand these aspects are important to game writing, you should consider showing that you're capable of doing them, and doing them well. Core scripted material—main narrative throughput and cut scenes—is important for showing you can write the "big stuff." But what's potentially just as important is fleshing out the range of material in your portfolio. Think about writing a goodly chunk of systemic dialogue, to demonstrate A) that you can do it and B) that you don't think it's beneath you. Consider writing character designs and world-building documents—within a reasonable length—to show you can create material that can be successfully handed off to other members of the team for them to use. Concision and understanding what details others need to work are key here; save the more writerly touches for another time. (Side note: This also does *not* mean info-dumping the six gigs' worth of material you worked up on your college D&D campaign that you're dying to share with the world. The world in general, and prospective employers in particular, are almost certainly not interested.) Include material that is appropriate for the company you are applying to, which allows you to demonstrate your knowledge of their subject matter. Finally, above all, you need to understand that your portfolio is an ever-evolving beast. As you get better, your portfolio should get better. Target its contents to the company you're talking with. And never be afraid to update, edit, or improve it.

Bob Bates (1986, Chief Creative Officer, External Studios, Zynga): Your portfolio should demonstrate that you have mastered multiple styles. For dialogue, it is vital to show that you can write succinctly (also called *writing short*). Gamers hate to read. Ideally, every dialogue line should fulfill four functions: reveal character, advance the story, convey information, and entertain. For exposition, you *still*  have to write short. No page-long descriptions of background and character—get it done in one paragraph, preferably in fewer than three sentences. Show you can be concise, entertaining, and coherent, and you might get the chance to become a bit-stained wretch.

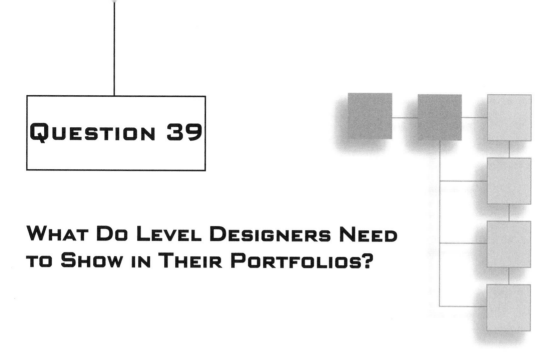

QUESTION 39

WHAT DO LEVEL DESIGNERS NEED TO SHOW IN THEIR PORTFOLIOS?

Brenda: Over the years, the term "level design" has evolved to mean "FPS level design." When one says they are a "level designer," that is generally what they mean. Level design, in reality, is so much more. For instance, in the role playing games I worked on, I did a lot of level design. My levels weren't designed for speed runs, offense, or defense, but were designed for puzzles, to mimic the personality of the level's builders (in narrative, anyway), or to fit a geographic area an NPC race inhabited. When looking at level designer portfolios, I look for the following:

- A fully playable and complete level with gameplay ready to go.

- Video walkthroughs of levels you have designed.

- Sketches of map layouts with detailed explanations of player experience, including all trigger points, spawn points, and so on.

- A mention of the software used.

- Proficiency in the level editor of the studio you're applying to, if at all possible.

- Content appropriateness. Do not include levels with naked people with questionable content, unless the company has published levels that include naked people and questionable content.

- Show work only if it looks like it was created by a senior level designer. Don't think you can get away with looking like a junior.

- Don't blame the tools. Making subpar stuff because "it was all the tools let you do" is an excuse certain to get you booted from consideration.

- Show evidence of great problem solving, careful execution and clear, succinct documentation of ideas and process.

- Remember that your website is an example in and of itself. If this is how you show yourself off, what are you going to do to my game?

Julian Widdows (1996, Vice President Development, Codemasters): Here are my thoughts based on six years of hiring designers and building a design team back at Rage/Swordfish Studios:

- **Passion and attitude:** A very positive attitude/outlook, a passion for level design, and the ability to talk around the idea that level designers are "experience architects," and as such are a key element of any shooter team/process.

- **Modeling ability:** Some evidence of technical modeling ability, ideally with one or more playable levels in their portfolio demonstrating a range of skills building single player and multiplayer levels.

- **In-game spatial awareness:** The ability to think in 3D, demonstrating the capability to create spaces that have well thought through verticality as well as horizontal movement. The most common problem I encountered with all level designers, entry level or not, was to map in 2D and then create a 3D space that felt like an extruded 2D map with very straight lines and a flat floor plane.

- **Some conceptual understanding of the importance of interesting traversal:** When prompted, higher-order thinking, such as the ability to take a conceptual space and choose an interesting means of traversal through this space, is important. Normally evidencing: The avoidance of doors except for specific dramatic effect; appropriate verticality; avoidance of symmetrical room entry and traversal except for specific dramatic effect; use of landmarks, handrails, and leading lines; surprising navigation;

surprising, varied, and interesting gameplay ideas/set pieces that support and build on the core mechanics, and offer lots of variety.

- **Communication:** Clear, concise, and passionate communication skills.
- **Geekery:** General wider geekery is always appreciated—passions for film, architecture, experience design, product design, storytelling are always appreciated, although not often in evidence.

We *always* tested our candidates. Using Sketchup, our workflow's primary ideation tool, we gave them a very detailed brief and two weeks in which to create an "ideation" model, with as much access to a mentor as they needed. This was completed in their own time, wherever they wanted, but not on site with us. Although a visually appealing level was a plus, we were looking for the skills mentioned previously more than anything.

For entry-level candidates, we did not look for specific scripting language experience, or indeed an understanding of design templates, metrics, and other more technical skills. Mostly we found this could be taught, although we did look for a good basic level of intelligence. A good degree was preferred, although not often in evidence for level design roles.

Zach Ford (2006, Level Designer, Gearbox): When looking at an entry-level level designer as a potential candidate for employment, I look for many qualities. First and foremost, a level designer needs to have passion and excitement about playing and creating games. Designers who play games make the best designs!

When I review candidates for Gearbox, I like to see what kind of work an applicant has done outside of school assignments or in their free time. It's a huge bonus to see levels in a portfolio that were created for a mod community. Seeing what work the applicant has done in their spare time is a window into seeing what passions they have, and it can show what type of games they are passionate about. Most importantly, it shows a level of personal drive that I find particularly exciting.

When I look at an applicant's levels, I look for level design foundations. Does the applicant have an understanding of how to create believable environments? Do these environments have a good flow that naturally draws players through them? It's particularly awesome to see when players inject a bit of storytelling into their environments. Does the applicant know how to use the environment to create interesting combat encounters? Are enemies introduced in an interesting way? I also like to see when applicants show an understanding of combat pacing because it's important for entry-level designers to have a foundation of core level design skills.

Lastly, good communication skills are a quality that everyone needs to have no matter what job you're applying for. Knowing how to collaborate with other people in and out of your department makes for stronger game development. Clearly communicating ideas can excite people, creating some of the most memorable moments in games.

Hiring entry-level level designers is always an exciting opportunity. We get to see an abundance of excitement from applicants breaking into the industry! At Gearbox, I hire designers who show their passion by constantly creating environments with solid level design practices and show a passion that's impossible to contain.

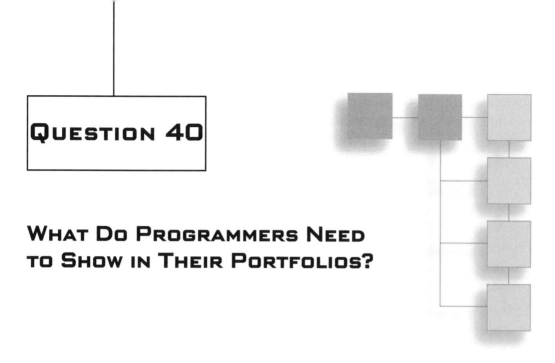

QUESTION 40

WHAT DO PROGRAMMERS NEED TO SHOW IN THEIR PORTFOLIOS?

Brenda: Coders should always have these things in their portfolios, although all may not be available readily (meaning potential employers often need to ask for them):

- Games (including source for non-commercial titles)
- Sample code in a variety of languages
- Clear commenting

Some coders have impressed other coders by arriving with an actual binder containing code samples that coders could review as well as the same code viewable on a laptop or iPad.

Often, coders are instead asked to complete a coding test (see Questions 58–60). If at all possible, see whether you can determine the bracing style of the company you're interviewing with. Much of the game industry uses aligned braces while many companies in the social space use K&R bracing. Coders generally have a very strong preference one way or another, so if you match their preference, so much the better.

Ian: Of course, what Brenda fails to mention is how she accidentally cost hours of productivity to a whole lot of programmers by innocently asking what bracing style they used, and triggering a holy war. Other questions that do this include preferred scripting language, variable naming conventions (to Hungarian or not to Hungarian?), and favorite platform/OS to develop for. Although you are free to have your own personal preferences, be prepared to learn and write in the style of the company you are going to work for. If you get a coding test, asking about preferred coding style is not a terrible idea.

Marq Singer (1999, Software Engineer, Freelance): When I'm purely looking at résumés, computer languages are probably the last thing I look at. The two things I most want to see in terms of formal course-work are a data structures class and some sort of team software engineering class. The latter teaches almost nothing about programming and everything about production process, beginning to end. Outside of a CS back-ground, I want to see a lot of math and physics. An old boss of mine once said he'd far rather teach a physicist to program than to try the other way around.

Now to portfolios, seeing as that's what you actually asked about. You'll drive yourself mad trying figure out what's going to impress which engineering director at which company, but there are some decent rules of thumb. First and foremost, show me a completed game/tool/whatever. Make sure it works beginning to end and is as bug-free as possible. Showing me that you can take something to completion means a lot more than any technical skill that will develop as time goes. With that in mind, don't just rehash/remake something that's been done before. No one wants to look at another *Tetris* clone ... especially if they've taught any game dev courses. Inspiration is fine, and if you think you have a compelling twist on an old title, go for it, but make sure it really is as interesting as you think. In that same vein ... *please* don't make some ginormous epic creation with 400+ hours of gameplay. You'll either never finish it, or it will be too detailed for a potential employer to get the gist of in a short time, or both ... probably both. An even more common mistake deserving of a strong warning: No multi-player; it's a lot harder than you think. And again, it's likely that only a single person will be looking at this. If all the cool stuff is in the multi-player function, it may never show.

With all of these caveats, there's still a lot of fun stuff you can do. Puzzle games are often easy to imagine, but hard to balance. The nice thing is that time spent in balancing will show. Humor is always good. If your game is simple and really only has one goal, make it a punch-line. If you're a bit too left-brained to make a compelling enough mini-game, design a tool. Take some horrid, repetitive task and automate it. Use a common set of mind-numbingly complicated data and visualize it so that it's understandable by someone who doesn't have a PhD in quantum mechanics. Make a Photoshop plug-in so useful that artists sing the praises of your name, throw flowers at your feet, and dedicate a national holiday in your honor. Okay, perhaps that's a bit much, but I'm sure you're up to it.

The main thing is, work within your strengths. If you're not a 3D type, sprites are perfectly fine. If UI isn't your strong suit, put in the minimum necessary. It's very possible to showcase a number of talents, no matter what your skill level.

Oh yeah . . . and after you've done all this, find the pieces of code you think are the most clever and/or relevant and put them into one document. People may want to see the whole codebase, but a highlights file helps a lot. Pretend you're still in school and comment the heck out of it. If your code is in something that isn't C/C++ or doesn't look a whole lot like it, comment twice as much. There's a good chance the person reviewing it may not know that particular language. The same goes with mods. A lot of companies use the Unreal engine, but a lot more don't.

The last bit of advice is to get a lot of feedback on your portfolio pieces, before and after applying. If you have friends who are coders, have them give you a formal code review. For the friends who don't have the technical background, have them actually use the software. It is almost assured that they'll break it in five minutes and not be able to figure out features you thought were intuitively obvious. After a submission/interview, if you don't make it, ask for some pointers to improve your portfolio. Not everyone has the time to answer questions from candidates. However, from my perspective, it's really hard to find qualified people. If my feedback results in a hirable candidate six months down the line, it's worth taking a few minutes to give some critique.

Mike Acton (1995, Engine Director, Insomniac): I don't often get portfolios from programmers, actually. At least not in the traditional sense of a package of items that I can look through to help make my decision about whether to look at this person further. However, I'll answer in what I believe is the spirit of the question: What should someone send to me (or others) when they are looking to join a team? But before I get to that, I'd like to make one point perfectly clear: The process is not fair. There is no secret formula. You can be the right person at the wrong time. You can get someone on a bad or busy day. No matter what, know that whether or not you get that job is not a reflection of you. You need to be persistent and always do work you can believe in. Which also brings me to the point. Show me what you believe in. Don't regurgitate what you learned in school. Don't tell me what you think I want to hear based on what *I've* written. Show me who *you* are. That

makes a great portfolio. In practice, have a website. Help me find you on Google. Have a point of view. Do projects at home and share them with the world. Post some code. Make lots of mistakes and talk about them. Show your love and your passion and you will stand out. And just keep at it. Every day. Forever and ever. Until you die.

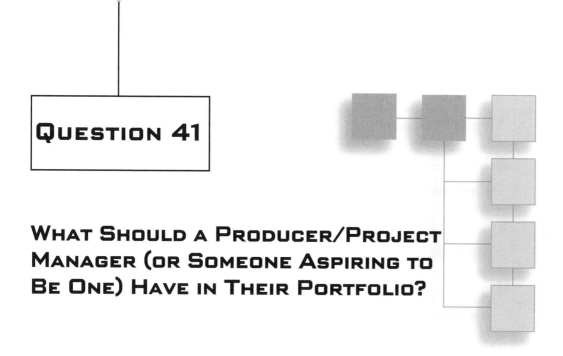

QUESTION 41

WHAT SHOULD A PRODUCER/PROJECT MANAGER (OR SOMEONE ASPIRING TO BE ONE) HAVE IN THEIR PORTFOLIO?

Brenda: A product manager (social game industry) and a producer (traditional game industry) share many of the same tasks: scheduling, managing the relationship between the team and the powers that be (the publisher, executive producer, marketers, and so on), managing the relationship between the team leads, and constantly pushing toward a release candidate. These are, of course, just a handful of the tasks these men and women take on. In the social space, the product manager (PM) is often responsible for handling the virality and improving monetization as well. Sometimes, the PM is the one responsible for designing the game, but if that's the route you want to go, become a game designer.

An experienced producer should, of course, show the games she's worked on. It's also useful to highlight companies if those companies are highly thought of for their ability to ship games of quality on time or have specialized production processes or methods. For those breaking into the industry, a production portfolio can be a bit more challenging. What do you show? Absent actual game development experience, there are a variety of things that would be of interest to prospective employers:

- Know the TRC, TCR, and platform policies. Each platform has specific policies that mandate certain behaviors of the games that run upon them. Knowledge of these policies is valuable.

- A certificate in project management available from a number of institutions.

- A role managing an event or a team or something that requires heavy management of time/resources. If you hosted, scheduled, and ran an event at your college for multiple years successfully, that would catch someone's eye.

- Regular, scheduled analysis of games on a blog that shows a level of dedication, your ability to plan and deploy a game, and your appreciation and understanding of a facet of the industry.

- Details on any project management software you've learned, with samples.

- Working within any community as a community manager, even as a volunteer.

- Guild leadership in MMOs.

- Running a successful small business, because if that doesn't require planning, nothing does.

- Evidence of familiarity with games in the selected genre. For instance, screen shots of your high-level avatar in all the popular social games shows that you're into it and get the medium.

- Evidence of great personal/interpersonal communications.

Karen Clark (2005, Director of Studio Operations, Loot Drop): Like a project manager, a producer's responsibilities include negotiation, mediation, problem-solving, and team-building. Like a product manager, the video game producer has the responsibility of making product-enhancing decisions such as identifying and removing under-performing aspects of a game. Sometimes he or she may expand tangential aspects into game-making features together with designers and other producers.

Generally, game producers don't build a portfolio. They aren't able to express their ability through digital media like an artist or level designer, nor are they able to share code snippets like a programmer. A producer could show project plans they drafted, or game design documents to which they have contributed. Unlike artists or programmers, the producer deals in intangibles: schedules, resources, plans, presentations, and other business collateral. The role they play is to broker ideas and keep morale high, to support the high-functioning team. Leadership, vision, and tenacity are the hallmarks of a good producer.

The most important attributes of a good producer are knowledge of standard production/project management practices in the game or software industry, experience leading teams and resolving conflict, and the ability to communicate to internal and external parties in business situations. Subject-matter expertise is not always needed, as the producer may be called upon to manage facets of a game without any prior knowledge. In the end, the producer must be able to walk into any situation, evaluate a problem, and take thoughtful action to remove roadblocks preventing successful completion of a game.

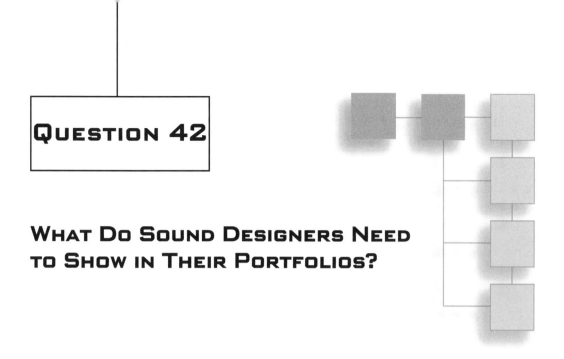

QUESTION 42

WHAT DO SOUND DESIGNERS NEED TO SHOW IN THEIR PORTFOLIOS?

Brenda: Sound represents one quarter of a player's experience. Tied together by code, sound, design, and art/UI work together to create a mood and a sense of tension or levity. Great sound makes a game. Increasingly, with the rise of both social and handheld games, options for sound designers are greater than they have ever been.

Zack Quarles (2000, Audio Director, id Software): When looking/listening to audio demo reels, my requirements are a bit different depending on the position/skill-level that I'm hiring for. There are some shared elements, though:

- **Practical in-game footage:** I'm really looking for a combination of great sound design and implementation. A sound designer has to be equal parts creative *and* technical. If you can make a really bitchin' sound effect, you'll have to do some legwork to make it sound equally bitchin' in a game environment.

- **Attention to detail:** Make sure you're thinking about *everything* in a scene. Ambience, environmental effects, hard effects, Foley, dialogue, dynamics, mix, and so on. As an audio professional, you're going to need to tell a story with your work. Make sure you're taking every element into account. Don't be lazy.

- **Ship something:** This can be either a big budget, Triple-A, retail project, or a MOD. I'm looking for someone who has the passion and commitment to games to the point that they will follow through. I generally gravitate to the MOD community anyway. By their very nature, there's a lot of "self-start" mentality with MOD teams. You definitely need that as an audio professional in the game industry.

▪ **Don't be an asshole:** I want to work with someone who takes pride in their work and understands that I have high standards for what I do and what I expect from audio professionals. On the other hand, I also want to be able to work with someone and not want to pull my hair out. At the end of the day, we're not curing cancer, we're making video games. Enjoy your work, enjoy the people you work with, and don't be a jerk.

So for me, it's equal parts talent/demo and drive/personality. If push comes to shove and I have the choice between two people—a great sound designer but sort of an ass or someone who really has passion and wants to do great work, but doesn't quite have the experience—I'll take the one that I might need to pull under my wing for a little while every time and not look back.

Dren McDonald (2009, Audio Lead, Nerdtracks): The opportunity to create audio for games has to rank up there as one of the best jobs ever. Most musicians I know have easily put off the wood-shedding of scales and patterns in exchange for "a few more kills" or to "just finish this level." As creative people, we are drawn to games, and honestly, what could be better than contributing to something we are so obsessed with?

Left brain/right brain—That obsession is certainly a trait of the right brain. Our imagination takes over, and in our mind we create the magical kingdom that is the game studio: where ogres, UFOs, and magical mushrooms roam the hallways. And there we are in the middle of it, with our keyboard, mics, and guitars, contributing to the fantasy. And hey, sometimes it kind of feels that way.

I think that one aspect of game audio that gets overlooked in our game studio fantasy is the fact that we're actually creating software: a very left-brained activity. Yes, you must create the ideal sound for that magical mushroom when it bursts into purple flames, but you also need to follow the correct naming convention in the filename, save it in the correct format, and commit that file to the correct directory. If you don't, you could break the game build, and all the ogres, fairies, and mushrooms quickly transform into very real looking pissed off people converging upon your audio oasis.

Finding a balance between being very creative and very technical can be challenging. Perhaps proving that you have that balance to others might be even more challenging. Oh, and in addition to that, you have to prove that you "work well with others." And it goes without saying that on the audio side, you can "bring it," and already have experience in creating quality audio files.

I've witnessed talented composers and sound designers alike throw up their hands at that point, shake their head, and admit defeat. I've seen it in emerging talent as well. But it's not all that much to overcome.

How do I get a job without experience?—The old chicken versus egg problem that faces many industries. Both the good and bad news is that there is no singular path. Here are some ideas:

- **If you are in school, go to IGDA meetings, campus programmer meetings, and so on, and find a way to meet other game enthusiasts.** Once you make some friends, set out to make your own game or make your own mod (there are many 'mod' teams out there creating versions of existing games). I know for a fact that Valve Software hired more than a couple dozen people there, solely because they worked on a successful mod team. In fact, one of those guys didn't set out to be an "audio guy" he just enjoyed being on the team and was going to law school. Valve called for the team to come work for them; he blew off law school and now makes weapon sounds for all the Valve stuff. Working on a team, be it a mod team or a simple team that creates an iPhone game, Flash game, and so on, shows others that you know how to work within a team, and you know the steps in building software. If you are an unknown composer, there is always a fear that you will be "difficult to work with" because composers can be notoriously ego driven, sensitive, defensive, and often oblivious to technical constraints. Don't be that guy/ girl, and show everyone that you aren't.

- **Create a video reel.** It's pretty easy these days to download some gameplay video and re-create the audio. If you are a sound designer, just do sound design. If you are a composer, do the music or team up with a sound designer. If you are a beginner, do several of these before you show one to a friend. After you've done a few for friends, consider posting them to your site (appropriately crediting the game and asking permission if necessary). Gameplay audio replacement is probably more valuable than cinematic audio replacement because it's a little tougher to make it realistic, but there's a higher payoff. Bonus: Create a reel that can showcase several genres: creature sounds, shooters, explosions, character sounds, footsteps, ambience, cute sounds, evil sounds, inventive sounds, and so on.

- **Be willing to do any job in games (especially when you are starting out).** A friend of mine who is a composer at LucasArts told me that after he went through the USC film/TV scoring program, he went to a large game company to do QA for almost a year, and that he considered that just as important as his time at USC. He soon landed the LucasArts gig after that. If you are a composer, don't be afraid to take a dialogue editing job, or a note tracking job for a music game. It's all experience.

- **Network, network, network!** The game industry is filled with people who love to chat about games or talk about projects they've worked on, and fortunately, most of them like to hear about what you've been working on or what your goals are. Coming from the music industry, I was completely shocked and pleasantly so when I discovered how friendly gaming folks are. When you go to an IGDA meeting, or GDC or a Game Dev meetup, everyone is there to talk and meet people. The best advice I heard about networking? "Don't show up thinking about what everyone there can do for you. Show up thinking about what you can do for them." And that doesn't only mean "I can offer you world class, fabulous audio!" That might mean "Oh, I also have some background in HTML if you need a hand with your website" or "Oh, have you met Linda over here with ReallyRad games? She's looking for a programmer with your background."

Patience is mandatory—All these little bits are the seeds you sow that take time to grow and form relationships and connections. If you keep at it, stay positive, and prove reliable, you will see results. I guarantee it. But this is assuming you've already been honing your audio skills, composing skills, know about gain staging, effects chains, EQ and compression, orchestral instrumentation, the Fletcher Munson curve, and a whole other host of audio knowledge . . . but that's another topic.

QUESTION 43

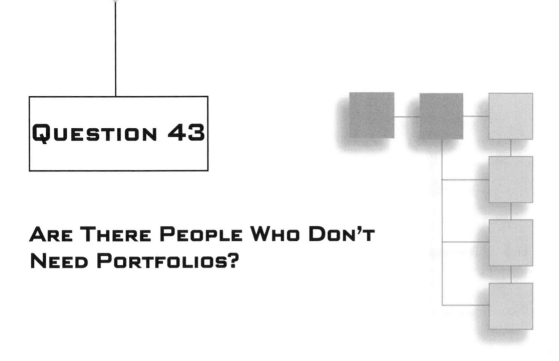

ARE THERE PEOPLE WHO DON'T NEED PORTFOLIOS?

Brenda: Sometimes, believe it or not, there are people who don't need portfolios. They come in several varieties:

- **Names**: These people have become famous in the industry for the work they have already completed. Their portfolio, in essence, has become a matter of public record. That record can work for and against you, of course.

Note

How can a person's record work against them? Consider the interesting case of John Romero. Romero designed and co-coded such landmark titles as *Wolfenstein 3D*, *DOOM*, and *Quake*, and created the FPS genre. In early 2010, when Romero wanted to break into the social games space, he found it challenging to do so. Most companies thought of him as merely "the guy who did shooters" despite the fact that his portfolio consists of over 130 games he'd created throughout the years. His shooter titles eclipsed all those other games. When Romero got the chance to design a social game, *Ravenwood Fair*, it quickly rose to become a huge hit on Facebook with nearly 12 million monthly players at its peak. He then went on to found his own social game company with me, Loot Drop. Romero also bears the legacy of the advertisement which was released for the shooter *Daikatana*. The ad, which featured the phrase, "John Romero's going to make you his bitch," was not created by Romero and he pushed back on its publication before finally letting his marketing exec release it. Nonetheless, the ad is what many people remember nowadays. Although most have not actually played the game (Romero still receives fan mail for it weekly), most critique the game harshly.

- **Super veterans:** Some people have been around a long time, and come with such a flotilla of references that a portfolio is an afterthought.

- **Leads/critical players on hit titles:** People who played a substantial role on a hit title often get in without a review of their previous work (or even a design, art or coding test, sometimes). This is extremely rare, though. In these cases, it's the game that's the "Name" versus the actual developer.

Each of these players has a *de facto* portfolio, of course. Mobygames.com provides a listing of many (hopefully all) of the games developers have been credited on. For many people in the game industry, a trip to mobygames.com is often the first stop when a candidate's résumé drops into the inbox.

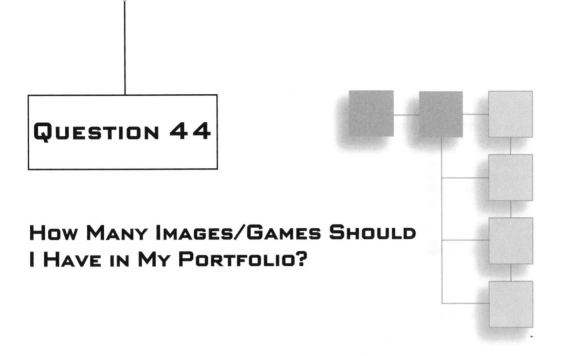

QUESTION 44

HOW MANY IMAGES/GAMES SHOULD I HAVE IN MY PORTFOLIO?

Brenda: A portfolio is not about quantity but about quality. Include only your best stuff. I have seen countless portfolios of students, and when I say, "That image there is kind of weak," the reply is commonly, "Well, I wanted to have *enough* images." Including "enough," however, is a huge mistake. First off, you are only as good as the weakest thing in your portfolio. Furthermore, no one reviewing your portfolio will know that Object Y was added to have "enough." In fact, they may have no way to differentiate it from the other projects. It's best to lead with your strongest stuff and stick to it. If you feel you need more things, then develop more greatness. Really, even a few amazing things are better than 10 so-so things. The guy who made *Minecraft*, Markus Persson, doesn't feel a need to list something *else* on his portfolio, I imagine.

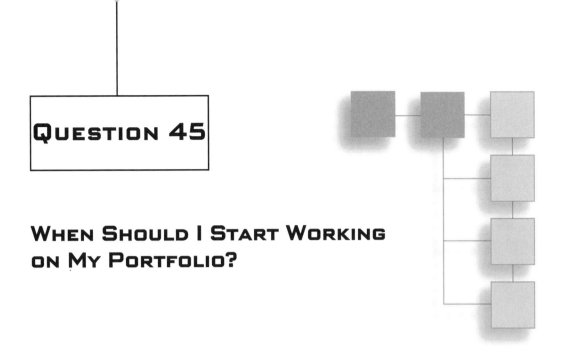

QUESTION 45

WHEN SHOULD I START WORKING ON MY PORTFOLIO?

Brenda: Now. You never know when opportunity will knock. One of the most common pitfalls people fall into both inside and outside the game industry is in letting their portfolio and their résumé slip. A typical college student, for instance, waits until their last quarter or semester in college before pulling a site together. However, it's often the case that recruiters from game companies began their visits in the fall. Having nothing prepared—or something hastily prepared—will rarely land you a job. What about the sophomore who suddenly finds herself talking with someone about a coding internship, but has no finished games to show?

It's a good idea for students to begin working on their portfolios the moment they believe they have something compelling for prospective employers to see. This accomplishes two tasks: One, it gets you job-focused and keeps you thinking about projects and pieces that you could work on and complete for your portfolio; and two, it means that if opportunity comes knocking, you are prepared.

Inside the industry, we face layoffs like everyone else, and the writing for said layoffs is often not on the wall. So, keeping your résumé and your portfolio up to date is important even when you have a job.

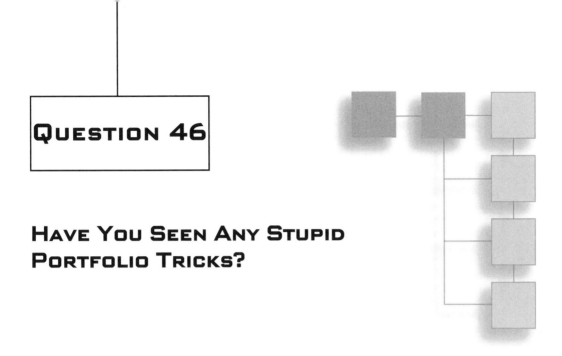

QUESTION 46

HAVE YOU SEEN ANY STUPID PORTFOLIO TRICKS?

Brenda: Yes, too many. Some of my favorites (and this is not a category in which one wants to be a "favorite") are as follows:

- **Under construction:** Don't suggest what you cannot show. It only further solidifies any suspicions people have about your ability to execute a concept to completion.

- **Dead blog:** Don't start a blog you don't have time to maintain. Odds are, whoever's reviewing your portfolio will not read it anyway.

- **Abstract thumbnails:** Show only obviously identifiable thumbnails. Showing the toe of a giant isn't nearly as interesting. Employers don't want to guess about what they're opening. They want to know.

- **Do not make your site a puzzle:** If you're a game designer, don't test me as a player. Don't make me work in the least little bit to get into your site.

- **Incorrect links:** Make sure to test your link from the e-mail/résumé you send. Sometimes, people misspell the link when they type it in, and although they have done everything to ensure their site is great, no one will actually see it because the link is broken. This is, of course, a separate case than the dead site, which is obviously bad for a host of reasons.

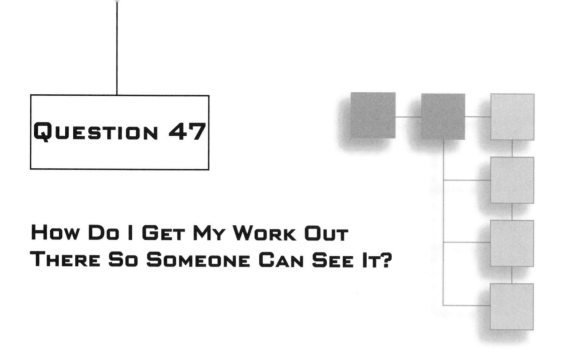

QUESTION 47

How Do I Get My Work Out There So Someone Can See It?

Ian: Start by putting it on your personal website. (If you do not have one of those, start by getting a personal website.) This will not get you much exposure, but it will at least make your work available to those who are specifically looking for it. Needless to say, put the URL on your business card.

If this is just portfolio work, like some stand-alone 3D models, you can nicely ask friends, colleagues, or others in your social network to visit your site and critique your work so that you can improve it. If you can talk critically about your work in a way that could help other students or professionals, thus becoming a useful resource in its own right, that would be an ideal situation.

Suppose you've made an actual *game*, either on your own or with others, and want to get it out there so people can play it and see how awesome you are. Depending on the platform, you can certainly upload it to game portals (there are a number of websites that will take your Flash game, for example, if you take a few simple steps to integrate your game with their API). If your game is really special, word of mouth can carry it to stardom if you're very lucky, but there is no guarantee here.

The next step is to enter your game in a contest such as IGF. In a contest where every game is played and judged on its merits, if your game truly stands out, it will be recognized. However, be realistic. Play winning games of previous years. Be honest with yourself about whether your work can reach that highest bar. If not, keep working on it (or start working on a new, better project). After all, you don't want exposure for something you made that is *mediocre* or *really bad*, do you? Before you spend time getting your game out there, make sure it's worth playing.

Brenda: In this day of social media, it seems the more challenging question is, "How do I keep it to myself?" The easiest way to promote yourself is to get a full web presence:

- Facebook account
- LinkedIn account
- Twitter account
- Blog or website

Next, learn to use each to bring people to your work. Begin with regularly posting new work or new writing for people, depending on your profession. Use Twitter, LinkedIn, and Facebook to direct people to your site when you post something new. Of course, it will take time to build up followers, but slowly, over time and through networking and providing information of value, you can build that network up. That said, bear in mind that you want to direct people toward good stuff, so it's wise to give it a first run in forums dedicated to peer critique. DeviantArt.com is a great site for just such a purpose. Peer critique groups for your discipline may also exist locally on or the Internet.

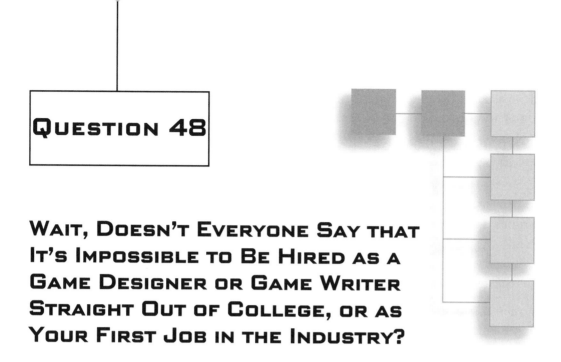

Question 48

Wait, Doesn't Everyone Say that It's Impossible to Be Hired as a Game Designer or Game Writer Straight Out of College, or as Your First Job in the Industry?

Ian: Yes, they do. And they're lying. But don't worry, it's for your own good. In reality, what people should say is that it is *very difficult* to get hired as a game designer or game writer with no prior industry experience, and that it is unlikely that this will happen for you. There are simply not that many entry-level game design or game writing jobs, and when one of them opens, there are a lot of applicants because these jobs are highly coveted. One of the authors of this book (not that author, the other one) got their first game design job after three years' industry experience as a game programmer, and this was for an entry-level, no-experience-necessary game design position. You will probably be competing with someone like that. Not to burst your bubble or anything.

That said, I've seen it happen plenty of times, so it is not impossible. By all means, if you have the skills and the desire, apply for any position that you are qualified for and that you really want. The worst thing that can happen is you get turned down, and you gain some extra job-hunting experience in the process.

If getting a game design job isn't impossible, why does everyone say so? Because they don't want you to depend on getting a design job right away. It might happen, but it might not, so have some kind of backup plan. Learn enough programming to get hired as a programmer, or learn enough art to get hired as an artist, or actually practice your communication skills and apply for QA jobs.

It's easier to change careers once you have industry experience, so give yourself as many possible points of entry as you can.

Scott Siegel (2006, Game Designer, Playdom/Disney): I moved to California from the East Coast in 2008 with no job prospects lined up. I knew that making games was my passion, and that New York City held no opportunities for an entry-level game designer with a liberal arts degree in Literature.

I spent three stress-filled months hopelessly hunting for jobs out West. Sent out loads of inquiries and took numerous unsuccessful interviews. Turns out my background as a blogger for Joystiq even made me ineligible for QA positions—I was assumed to be high-risk for leaked content. I worked on non-digital games for *The Escapist* on the side, kept blogging, developed an RSI, and started looking for jobs at my favorite local eateries.

When *Parking Wars* hit Facebook, I took notice, and started writing about the encroaching "social games" phenomenon. I attended the first ever Social Gaming Summit in San Francisco. I networked like crazy. Every exec who took the stage went on about how what they really needed were designers.

I attended the after-party at the Zynga offices. Grabbed a beer, but didn't drink it. Went up to the CEO, clinked bottles, and told him "I'm that game designer you're looking for." He immediately introduced me to a handful of his staff. Two weeks later, I started as a contract game designer at Zynga. In less than a month I converted to full-time. I've been making games for social networks ever since.

Will Kerslake (1998, Creative Director, Radar Group): My first job was at Atari in Milpitas in '98, which was old school console Atari Games not separate Atari Home → Hasboro → Infogames. I went to college at a tiny place in Sunnyvale called Cogswell knowing full well I wanted to make games. I was learning

3D art as it seemed to be the fastest path in during the mid/late 90s, plus the school's Bay Area location seemed like a good place to be for getting a job. I took over as the webmaster for the college and got a recruitment e-mail from Atari to put on the school's bulletin board. I posted it and made sure a few friends knew about the potential openings. One of them got a job there, and then he recommended me. I was hired a couple weeks later.

David Feltham (2000, Senior Designer, BioWare): It was 1999 and I had been working for three years in broadcast design—logos and openings for TV shows—and wanted to get into games. I was a gamer and was excited about the prospects of where the game industry was going. I had actually applied to BioWare and had a phone interview with Greg Zeschuck who, wisely, said that I would have to have more experience if I wanted to work for them. Then I got word from a networking contact who told me a small start-up game developer was making a game for a new console coming out. I applied for the position of 3D artist and six months later was hired creating and texturing props and placing them in levels for their game that would inevitably become *Cel Damage* for the Xbox and Gamecube.

We were a small company, so we all helped out in different areas: When we needed animation, I'd help out there because of my background in broadcast design. Eventually, we got bigger and needed a department focused solely on making levels, and I was made Lead Artist, basically the guy in charge of tracking the assets, maintaining consistency and quality, and being the go-between between Level Design and Level Art. I spent a lot of time helping out in both departments. We eventually shipped *Full Auto* (Xbox 360) and *Full Auto 2* (PS3). The company eventually folded, sadly, and I moved on. My former boss was now working for BioWare and was looking for Level Designers who had a background in Art to help bridge the gap between the two departments. I did an extensive test for them and after a few interviews was hired and moved my family out to Edmonton. I worked on *Mass Effect 2, Lair of the Shadowbroker,* and the project I'm working on now that I can't tell you about. I've been here coming up on four years.

Aaron Butler (2002, Game Designer, Insomniac Games): I broke into the gaming industry in 2002 when I was hired on as a Designer/QA at Black Ops Entertainment working on *Terminator 3: Rise of the Machines*. A friend of mine working at the studio got me an interview; they liked what they heard and brought me on. After a month or so, my skills as a designer were liked enough that I was made a full-time designer on *T3:RoTM,* and I've been a designer ever since. This is my dream job, and I consider myself fortunate that I get to do what I love for my career.

At the same time, I was also finishing up my first year at the Art Institute of California Los Angeles. I was part of the first class in their Game Art & Design program. My only "game industry" related experience before that was reviewing games for GameSpy.com and Game-Over.net, as well as a production internship at Atari Santa Monica.

Although I had been a gamer since the days of Atari, I feel the thing that helped me out the most in getting the design job was reviewing games. Taking my love of games and then analyzing and reviewing them allowed me to better understand how they were constructed.

QUESTION 49

HOW MUCH HELP WILL READING ABOUT GAME DEVELOPMENT BE IN OBTAINING A JOB IN THE GAME INDUSTRY?

Brenda: Reading about games is a part of your job both in the industry and as you prepare to enter it. It's critical to stay on top of the latest developments by reading game industry news and associated tech news. Many game devs have found that following press on Twitter greatly automates the process by having news pushed at you instead of having to go out and get it.

There are also a lot of books aimed at the various disciplines. These can be important, too. Some coders comb white papers, for instance, looking for new algorithms. Book stores have shelves stuffed with game books. My rule of thumb is this: If the book is written by someone with a background in the game industry and it deals with something I want to learn, I will pick it up.

Keep in mind that there is no book, no article, and no white paper that is a substitute for making games. Applied knowledge and finished games are still the most important things.

Ian: Just to restate Brenda's point, a lot of people are intimidated when they sit down to make a game. This is natural, and a rational-seeming line of reasoning might be that if you feel that way, you must not know enough to make games yet, so you read a book or some articles on a website, on the theory that you'll pick up whatever you don't realize you're missing, and that will enable you to get started.

This line of thinking is a trap. No amount of reading will *ever* get you over that feeling of fear. This is because this feeling doesn't actually come from a lack of knowledge, but a lack of experience. So what will happen (maybe this has happened to you already) is you'll read, you'll still feel intimidated, and then you'll figure that must not have been the right book, and you'll try reading something else.

Instead, work on overcoming your fear. Make a game, even if it's a bad one. If you don't know where to start, start by figuring out what you *can* do with your current skills: a simple roll-and-move, race-to-the-end board game? A re-themed clone of an existing game? It doesn't matter—just make something and take that project to completion. Then, reflect. Did you learn anything? What elements of your game could be better? What parts of the development process do you think you could handle more efficiently? Did you run into any obstacles where there were specific pieces of knowledge that you feel you're missing? If you've identified a *specific* skill that you're lacking, a targeted web or book search will be useful in finding articles or book chapters on that one thing you need.

Once you are over this initial fear and you're comfortable making games, you will probably find yourself reading books a lot more. You'll also enjoy the process more, because the things you're reading will be relevant to your existing experience. You can say "Oh, I remember running into that problem; this article gives a really interesting solution!" instead of just saying "Huh, that's … interesting. But it still doesn't tell me how to make games."

The astute reader might have noticed that Brenda and I have already published a book on game design, targeted to beginners: *Challenges for Game Designers*. If you have read that book, you'll notice that you cannot read very far without being asked to get off your butt and actually design some games. Now you know why we wrote it that way.

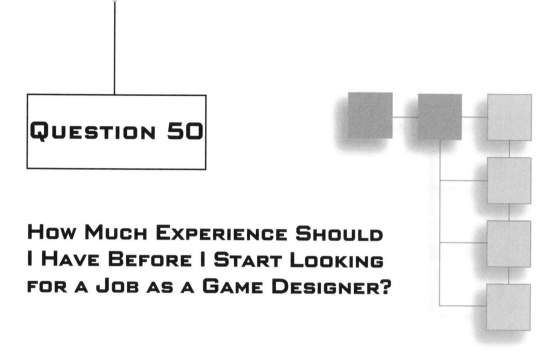

QUESTION 50

HOW MUCH EXPERIENCE SHOULD I HAVE BEFORE I START LOOKING FOR A JOB AS A GAME DESIGNER?

Brenda: This is a tricky question. Let me tell you about the last two interns I took on as well as a mentee I recently agreed to work with:

- **Intern 1:** A former student of mine had a degree in game design, was a solid writer, and good at taking direction. He wrote good design docs, but hadn't really proven himself with a fully functional game. He wrote to me asking me if I had an internship available to him. He made his case—his skills, how hard he was willing to work, that he'd work for peanuts if necessary. In short, his skills were known to me, and he removed as many barriers to his hiring as he possibly could. He also spoke to his sincere passion to break into the industry and assured me he'd work hard and not make me regret it.

- **Intern 2:** Someone who was not known to me personally or on social media (Twitter, Facebook, or what have you) wrote to me to express his desire to work with me at my current company, Loot Drop. He outlined his previous internship experience in games, noted that he'd work for peanuts and, again, took time to mention why he wanted an internship at Loot Drop specifically. He gave me a range of choices about what he could do—from coding to design—and left the options with me.

- **Mentee:** Someone I've met at a number of conferences and also talked with when she was a student contacted me via e-mail and asked me if I'd mentor her as she transitioned from industry coder to industry designer. Like the others, she laid out her case, expressed a willingness to work and promised to make it convenient to my schedule.

It wasn't until now in writing these events out that it occurred to me why all these instances worked while others had failed:

- **Unexpected:** None of the interns approached me when I was slogging through a wall of other intern résumés. Instead, they approached me and sold me on their skills in the absence of any real competition.

- **Personalized:** Each of them made it abundantly clear that the outreach was personal. I didn't feel like I was letter 2 of 20. It seemed very clear to me that their outreach was directed, knowledgeable, and personal.

- **Outlined skills:** They sold themselves and why they would be good for me or my company without overstating themselves. In the case of Intern 2, he was trying to come into a company where the average design experience was 26 years in the industry and the average coding experience was 27 years in the industry! So, in his case, he pointed out that his primary goal was to help wherever it would be useful given his previous experience in the social space while learning from the people here. Coming off as arrogant and overstating what you can contribute can turn potential opportunities into closed doors.

- **Demonstrated passion:** Every candidate expressed their love for games and desire to break into the industry (or a new discipline with the same industry). They showed they'd been working toward this point, not just asking for a lucky break. They showed me that they genuinely liked and played the kind of games I was currently making.

- **Minimized cost and minimum barriers:** They knew the barriers to entry—cost, time consumption, not enough for them to do, and low pay. Every intern I have hired ultimately converted to a regularly paid employee. In the beginning, though, they all worked for $10 an hour just for the experience.

Start working now to get that game development job. Take on volunteer roles in guilds, game communities, and the like. Do what you can do at game jams to get some experience under your belt. Start coding and start making games!

Ian: If this is the career path you want, start applying as soon as you are prepared to do the job. You may not get the first job you apply to (or the second, or the tenth …) so start as early as you are ready. In the meantime, keep working on your skills (in other words, design games on your own time) so that future job applications will be more likely to get you there. It often takes a while, especially if you have no previous work experience as a designer, so be prepared for the long haul and understand that rejection form letters are part of the process and not the "you can't do this, go away" warning that they sometimes feel like.

When finding any job in the industry (but especially design), there is a tradeoff between time and requirements: The more you demand, the more time it will take. Are you unwilling to move to a new country (or even to another city within your home country)? Do you have minimum salary requirements? Do you only want to work on certain kinds of games or at specific kinds of companies? Or are you open to just about anything? Basically, the more constraints, the fewer opportunities that will match, which means there will be fewer jobs that you can apply for, which means it will take longer for you to find the one that will accept you. The more you can put up with, the less you'll have to wait.

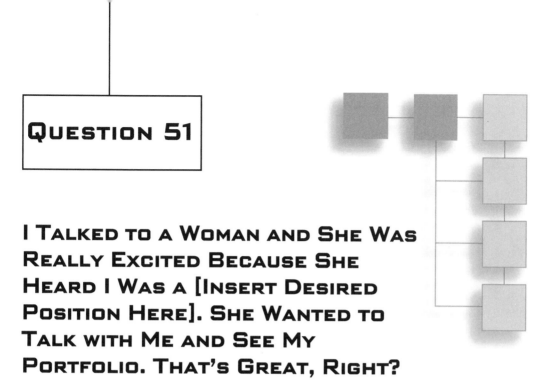

QUESTION 51

I Talked to a Woman and She Was Really Excited Because She Heard I Was a [Insert Desired Position Here]. She Wanted to Talk with Me and See My Portfolio. That's Great, Right?

Brenda: Hardly. If she sees your portfolio and still wants to talk with you, that's better. If she hires you, that's great. A lot of times, prospective game developers meet independent recruiters, HR representatives of game companies or their employees and assume that their friendly demeanor and initial positive response is a signal that things could be great for them. As you're sitting there, it may seem obvious to think, "Well, no kidding!" However, when you're the one who's just finished an extremely positive 15-minute conversation with a recruiter from [insert dream company here], it's hard to remain objective. First of all, people mistake friendliness for confidence in their caliber as a potential employee. Secondly, people mistake willingness to look at a portfolio or eagerness to fulfill a role as eagerness to get them into that role. Remind yourself to remain objective, but if you have that opportunity to show off a great portfolio, by all means, show it!

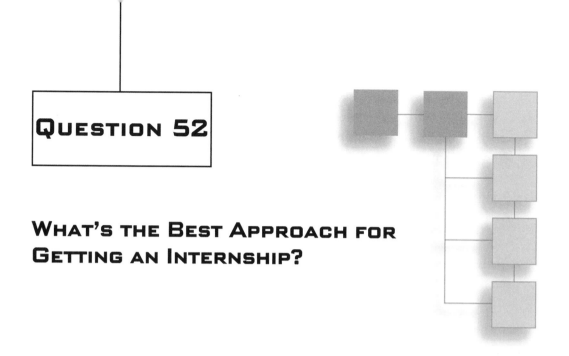

QUESTION 52

WHAT'S THE BEST APPROACH FOR GETTING AN INTERNSHIP?

Ian: See Brenda's answer to Question 50 for some examples of interns she has hired, and why she hired them. As for me, I posted this on my blog (http://teachingdesign.blogspot.com/2009/02/summer-internships.html), which I am reprinting here with permission from myself.

First, let me say that *internships in the game industry are rare.* This is not about game companies being mean, or hating students. It's because game projects typically take longer than a summer, and development teams don't particularly like it when a key project member leaves in mid-project. It also takes people time to ramp up, which means just around the time that interns are finally able to contribute something to the team, they leave. Also, interns take a lot of management time that a typically overworked producer does not have, so many studios decide that it's just not worth it.

This is not to say that internships don't exist, merely that the companies that offer them tend to be low-key about it (lest they be flooded with tens of thousands of résumés from eager college students). That means they aren't advertising, so you have to find them other ways (see next).

My advice to students seeking summer employment:

- **First, do your homework.** Research a lot of game companies, go to their corporate websites and see if they have internship programs. Your best bets are local companies, since realistically you aren't going to get housing or relocation expenses (some companies won't even *consider* you for an internship unless you live in the area). Be willing to look at lesser-known companies (not just the big names that you drool over), and look in related fields like serious games—fewer students are looking there, so there's less competition.

■ **How do you find local developers?** First, check GameDevMap.com. Second, check if there's a local IGDA chapter. Third, check Google with a search string that searches for game developers in your local area. Fourth, check with your school's career services office... but you probably won't find anything there that you couldn't have found on your own, which is why I list it last.

Some "internships" may not be listed as such; rather, they may be called "QA" positions that just happen to span the summer term.

■ **If you can't find anything in games, consider a related industry.** Programmers can do a programming internship at *any* software company and still gain valuable experience. Artists can work in fields like advertising or industrial design.

■ **If you absolutely can't find any paid work, finances permitting, "hire" yourself full-time to work on your own game projects!** Force yourself to work 40+ hours per week on your own game, as if you were at a full-time job. (This works even better if you have some friends you can team up with.) Keep your scope small, so that your projects are achievable. The point here isn't to "start a game company" or "make a great game and sell it"—the point is to get valuable experience making games. If your project sucks, that's fine, as long as you *learned something* from the process. If your project *does* end up being awesome, enter it in a contest such as the IGF Student Showcase, which is just as juicy a résumé builder as an internship (if you win).

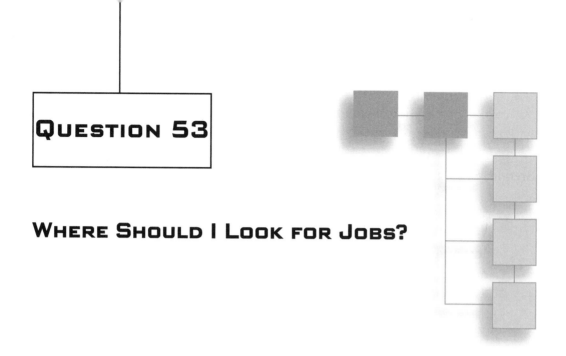

QUESTION 53

WHERE SHOULD I LOOK FOR JOBS?

Ian: Everywhere! Some useful resources include:

- **Social networks.** Especially if you already know people in the industry. Follow people you admire (many have blogs, or Twitter, or both), as they will occasionally post that they are looking to hire. In addition, the Twitter hashtag #gamejobs has evolved and includes lots of postings every day.

- **Local game industry meetups.** There's no shame in showing up at an informal gathering of developers and mentioning that you're looking for work; many such groups consider it their primary reason for existence.

- **Game industry conferences.** Aside from meeting people who are hiring through chance encounters, many conferences have some kind of career track or career expo where you can talk directly to hiring managers at game companies that are specifically looking to hire.

- **Industry-specific online job boards.** More general job websites are not particularly useful, and stay away from any job postings that require you to pay in order to view or apply for jobs (those tend to be scams), but there are some places where game companies post their open jobs.

- **Game company websites.** Is there a specific list of companies you would love to work at? Browse around the corporate websites; many companies maintain an up-to-date list of job postings right there.

Brenda: Some more bonus listings to round out Ian's list:

- **Craigslist.org.** Major game industry hubs like San Francisco make use of Craigslist heavily for job postings.

- **Industry-specific websites.** Sites like Gamasutra.com and InsideSocial Games.com have great listings of available jobs, and they're just the tip of the iceberg. Often, these jobs are for more experienced talent.

- **Make yourself known.** Follow people on Twitter and ping them regularly (a couple times a month) with quick, intelligent comments or questions that don't require a massive e-mail or multiple tweets to answer. The point isn't to irritate the developer, but to make yourself known to him or her. I have gotten to know multiple newcomers through Twitter and have hired four people based on Twitter posts in the last six months alone. I find it is the easiest way to source the help I need.

- **Know others.** Particularly at game conferences, know who you're standing next to. From three floors up, I watched a former student stand casually next to Peter Molyneux. He made quick chat with him, but it seemed cut short. Turns out, he had no idea who he was next to. Don't blow your chances.

- **Ask.** I actually hired one person into a paid internship and then a junior designer position because they wrote me and asked me if I would give them a chance. They had a good portfolio of work and genuine passion, so I did. Bear in mind, approaching your favorite developer at GDC and asking for a job is not recommended if you don't have an existing relationship. If you don't know a person, ask by e-mail, not in person.

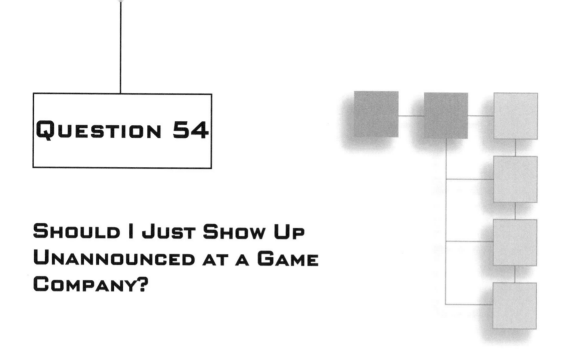

Question 54

Should I Just Show Up Unannounced at a Game Company?

Ian: Not unless you want to embarrass yourself and make other people hate you. Game developers are friendly as a whole under normal conditions, but they tend to be very busy, *especially* when at work. If you show up unannounced, it's very likely that no one will have the time to even say hi to you, and you'll be asked nicely to leave by whomever happens to be nearest the front desk. Look at it from the company's perspective: You are interrupting their work, slowing them down, and therefore making their game that much less fun/good/profitable. Would *you* want to hire someone who showed such disregard for the work you do?

Brenda: This is a generally accepted no-no. If you do this, it's basically saying, "I really don't have a clue about how this works. Please, remember me for my thoughtlessness." Based on seeing the after-effects of this happening at a game company, people will also say unflattering things about you when you leave.

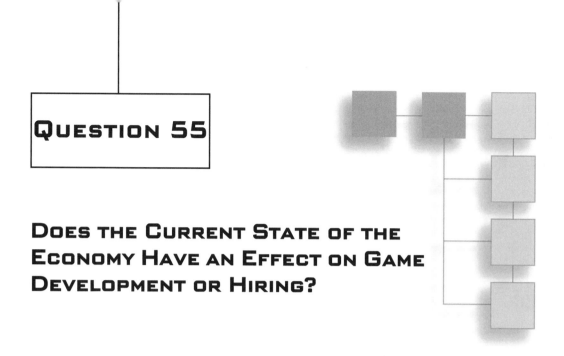

QUESTION 55

DOES THE CURRENT STATE OF THE ECONOMY HAVE AN EFFECT ON GAME DEVELOPMENT OR HIRING?

Ian: Of course it does. The game industry doesn't exist in some kind of alternate universe. The laws of physics and economics still apply.

But then, this doesn't really matter. It's a factor beyond your control (if global economic conditions *are* under your control, stop reading this and start your own game company). Anyway, conditions change so rapidly and unpredictably that long-term planning is meaningless. Yesterday's hiring freeze may turn into today's hiring spree and tomorrow's massive layoffs. If you have a true passion for game development, find a way to do what you love to do. Don't stay away because you're scared of the economy. And whatever you do, don't seek out this line of work if you don't love it, no matter what the job prospects seem to be.

What do you do if you just happen to be trying to get a job at a time when the hiring situation is nonexistent? One thing to remember is that the game industry is fragmented, and a market crash in one space may mean open opportunities in another. In the year 2010, AAA companies were laying off employees left and right, at the same time that the social game developers were hiring everyone they could get their hands on. A few years before that, it was serious game companies struggling to hire enough developers to fill their ranks, and a few years before that it was the MMO companies. Be on the lookout for opportunities in all of the nooks and crannies of the industry, not just traditional big-budget PC or console development, and you may find a lot more opportunity than you originally thought.

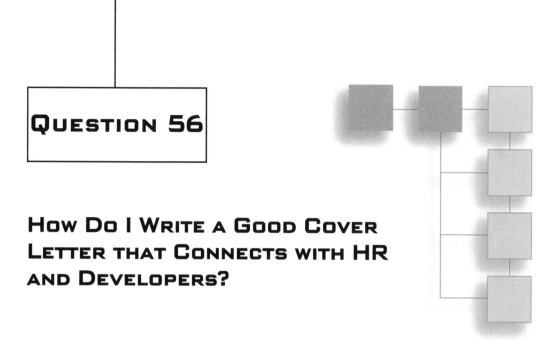

QUESTION 56

HOW DO I WRITE A GOOD COVER LETTER THAT CONNECTS WITH HR AND DEVELOPERS?

Brenda: There is no one perfect cover letter for a company or for a single individual. There are hundreds on the Internet you can review to get an idea of what's right for you. In general, cover letters need to follow this basic format:

- **First paragraph:** Note which job you're applying for.

- **Second paragraph:** Note why you're good for it; mention key skills, awards, and recently released projects. Use more paragraphs if necessary.

- **Third paragraph:** Encourage them to contact you and provide the means to make that contact happen.

Don't go overboard in length, though. If your cover letter is long, people are going to flip right past it (or the e-mail) and read (click on) the résumé you attached first instead. So, keep it as short as possible.

Within the body of the letter, you need to demonstrate:

- **Knowledge of the company/personalization:** No one likes a form letter. In fact, I know of game developers who just toss them away! Take the time to make your approach a customized one.

- **Show you can do the job:** Note the experience you have that relates to the job. If you have any special awards or are a veteran of the game industry, say so.

- **Professionalism:** Be sure to proofread your letter and have others proofread it, too. If you are sloppy when presenting yourself, what are you going to do inside the company? Don't risk the chance that it will matter to them.

Ian: Writing cover letters for the game industry is pretty similar to writing cover letters for any other industry, so most of the general "career" advice you read in books or online applies here as well.

Since games are a casual industry in many ways, you might be tempted to make your cover letter gimmicky or overly conversational in tone. This is a huge risk; if you hit just the right note that resonates with the company's culture, it can get you noticed ... but any misstep and you'll be eliminated. I would not attempt this; the risks far outweigh the benefits. Let your qualifications speak for themselves, without using special gimmicks that make it look like you're trying to distract the reader away from the skills that they should be hiring you for.

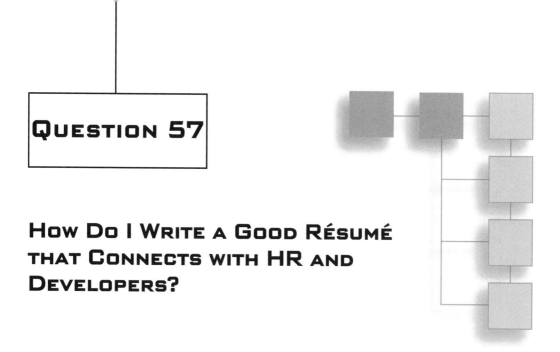

QUESTION 57

HOW DO I WRITE A GOOD RÉSUMÉ THAT CONNECTS WITH HR AND DEVELOPERS?

Brenda: A résumé is often the first thing that anyone looks at, so it has to be good. I have often referred to it as a "$50,000 piece of paper," because in many cases, that is exactly what it is. That résumé is trying to sell you into a gig that will hopefully make you that much or more. Typos, inaccuracies, or things that are not clear may cost you a job.

When prospective employers look through a résumé, these are the things they need to see:

- **A clear objective line:** Let me know precisely which job or range of jobs you are applying for. Often, these are listed on the company's job page. If you are qualified for more than one, include both or state your flexibility by saying, for example, "a programming position." Whatever you do, don't make the employer do the work or think that it will be blindly obvious. Often it's not, and unless you're a rock star candidate, people may not invest time in the investigation. I find it also helps to list your time in the industry if you have 10+ years in. "Veteran game programmer ..." or "Designer with 20+ years experience seeks ...". This moves your résumé to the top of the pile. Don't add these monikers if you don't have 10+ years, though. Adding "Experienced coder ..." is fine provided you do indeed have a published title or two under your belt.

173

- **A list of pertinent software/languages/skills:** List the coding languages or pertinent programs you know well. For instance, coders should list C/C++ and the like. Artists should include details of the graphics packages they know well, such as Maya or 3DS Max. If you have specific talents like 2D animation or system design, this is also a key place to list those.

- **A list of relevant jobs:** List only jobs that are relevant to the position for which you are applying. Hopefully, you have scored an internship or a volunteer gig which you can list. Next on the totem pole would be experience working with a mod group. The more experience and the more prominent the better. If you have no game industry experience, you can list your regular working experience. I have also seen students list student projects with made up studio names (the studio name was something they selected in school).

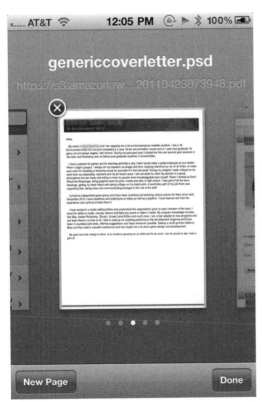

Avoid filenames that reveal a mass-mailing approach to job search!

Inevitably, this just comes across as misleading to me and to the other developers I spoke to. If you must list them, be sure it clearly delineates the work as part of a student project.

- **Clear ways to contact you:** Provide your e-mail, phone number, and a link to your online portfolio.

- **Customized approach:** In everything in your résumé, it should be clear why you are contacting the company. It's surprising the number of résumés that I see that fairly well scream "I make console games" when they're applying for a spot in a social game company. Making the leap is actually fine, but at least explain that this is what you're doing, hopefully in the objective line. Otherwise, it may appear that you're just shooting your résumé out scattershot.

- **Give it a good filename:** When sending your résumé to people, make sure the name of the file is customized, provided they would ever see that (and if you upload it, assume they will). Nothing says, "I really want this" like GenericCoverLetter.doc.

Ian: Remember that your audience is a stressed hiring manager looking at a massive stack of applications, with limited time to fill a critical position. Make their work as easy as possible, which means making your résumé as easy to read as you can. Aside from making sure you proofread it, this also means ordering the sections from most to least relevant. The first thing they're going to want to know is what position you're applying for ("objective"), so put that first. If you have industry experience, that is probably the next most important thing about your work background they will want to know, so put the games you worked on and companies you worked for next. If you are a student with no experience, your skills, relevant coursework, and degree are probably the most important things about you.

Basically, write all of the sections, and then order them from top to bottom in order of importance. Ask yourself, if you could show the hiring manager only one section of your résumé, which section would it be? Put that at the top, and then repeat the process for the remaining sections.

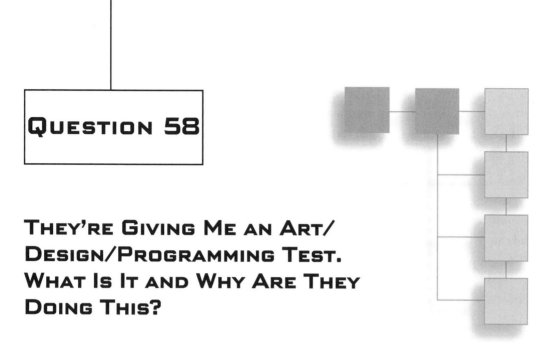

QUESTION 58

THEY'RE GIVING ME AN ART/ DESIGN/PROGRAMMING TEST. WHAT IS IT AND WHY ARE THEY DOING THIS?

Ian: Your cover letter and résumé show that you have experience. Your portfolio or work samples show that you have skills. But one thing that the company you're applying to still doesn't know about you is how you'll react to the specific nature of work that they do there ... they don't just want to know what your past work looks like; they'd like to know what your future work will look like as well. One way of doing this is to ask you to perform some small-scale task: Write some code to a given spec, create a model from a reference photo, design a particular kind of game system, and so on. These tasks may be similar in nature to what you'd be doing on the job, so pay attention to whether this is the kind of thing you'd like to do for 70 hours each week. On the other hand, they may be merely tests to determine your skill with a particular language or provide your prospective employer with an insight into how you solve problems.

Once a company has received your résumé and cover letter and decided they want to interview you, they may respond not only with an interview request, but also with a test for you. The length of time you have to complete a test varies. Generally, coding tests are timed. You may have as little as one hour from the time of receipt to complete a specific assignment. Design and art tests take longer, usually one day for a design test and one week for an art test. More rarely, a company may ask you to submit a test as part of your application. In either case, your test will be a talking point during the interview (or the reason you're not getting an interview). Expect to be asked a lot of questions and be critiqued on your test; this offers the company a chance to see not only your work, but also how you respond to criticism. Bring a copy of your test to the interview so that you're prepared to talk about it (and if it's not fresh in your mind, take some time the day before to refamiliarize yourself with your answers).

Brenda: A word of warning about this—plenty of eager potential developers have reached out to companies only to be hit with a landslide of potential opportunity. I recall one particular student who received three level design tests all due within a week—and that week happened to be finals week! Also, consider that company A won't take too kindly to you saying, "I need to finish this for company B first." Why not just come straight out and tell them they're your second choice?

In my position as a person who hires, I've seen some pretty surprising things—code cut and pasted off the 'net, obvious content omissions in design tests where the IP (intellectual property) was phenomenally obvious, and art styles that didn't match anything the company produced. When setting yourself up to take a test, make sure that you have stacked the odds on your side. Coders should have their coding environment ready to go. A timed test starts when you receive the test, not at your leisure. It is perfectly okay to send your test code back in and follow up shortly thereafter with an optimized version. One coder who applied to my company did this, adding better commenting and altering an algorithm to make it more efficient. He did this immediately after his test, so we could see that in 25 more minutes, he'd made that additional progress. It also let us know that he wanted to present himself in the best possible light. If your code doesn't work, don't assume that it's all over. That's not always the case. The best coding tests have many approaches, and the approach you take lets the employer know your aptitude level. If you don't finish the test, follow up with something that's functional as soon as possible.

Designers should be very familiar with the games of the company, and have them installed and ready to analyze. I was once given a design test where I was asked to create a design doc for the character creation system in the game. I had 24 hours in which to do it. Imagine if I had to buy the game, install the game, download the relevant patches, and so on. I could have left myself with a minimum amount of time to design, write, and proof my submission.

Fortunately, I didn't do that. Artists must familiarize themselves with the company's style. Literally, everything you need to know is right there in front of you.

The reality of tests is that they invariably make the good look better and the not-so-good look worse. They are necessary because of the inordinate amount of padding people give their résumés. If you know your stuff, don't be worried. Also, save yourself the strain and apply only to places where you really want to work and that are working on the games you want to work on. Otherwise, you're wasting your own time (and theirs).

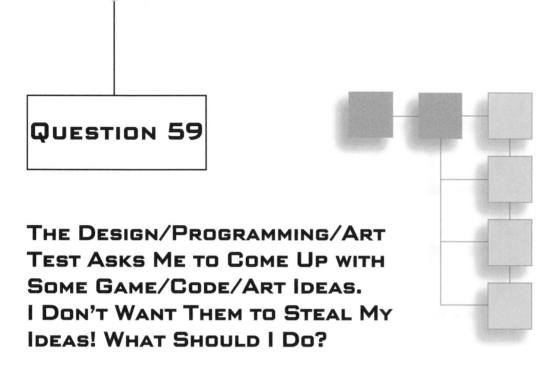

QUESTION 59

THE DESIGN/PROGRAMMING/ART TEST ASKS ME TO COME UP WITH SOME GAME/CODE/ART IDEAS. I DON'T WANT THEM TO STEAL MY IDEAS! WHAT SHOULD I DO?

Brenda: First off, relax. The game company is not going to steal your ideas. Every game company, nay, every game developer, has far more ideas than they have money and people to make them, so have no fear that this is merely a ploy to get free work from up-and-coming geniuses. In fact, if you do come up with something amazing and innovative, that will make them want you *and* your work. Rather, you need to prove yourself, and merely saying, "Oh, I can do it," doesn't prove that point. It's different when you have shipped titles. Even then, depending on the caliber of the game and the company you're hoping to work for, a design test may be necessary. For instance, after working on RPGs for nearly 20 years, I was still asked to submit a design test for a company. They were looking to hire me as lead on a live MMO, and they wanted to see if I could work within their world before we even spent time talking on the phone. It was a completely necessary and reasonable request. And no, they didn't "steal" my idea.

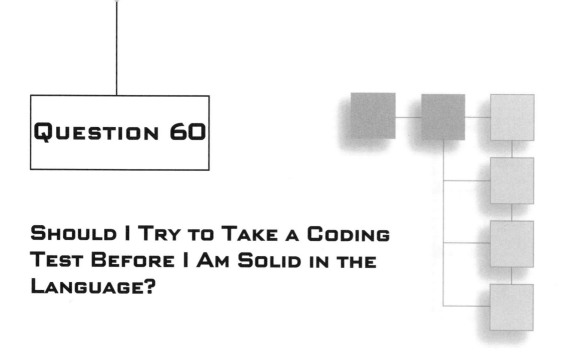

QUESTION 60

SHOULD I TRY TO TAKE A CODING TEST BEFORE I AM SOLID IN THE LANGUAGE?

Brenda: For the love of all you hold dear, no. In the last year, we've noticed a rash of programmers submitting their résumés to companies before they really should have, and the reality for many of those coders is that they just blew their one and only shot. Once a company has given a coding test to a candidate, they are unlikely to do so again in the near future. Once failed, so the mantra goes, why bother?

Coding tests at game companies aren't designed to test proficiency—they are designed for one of two things—to test mastery or to test skill level for lower level positions, and the lowest-level industry position is nothing to sneeze at.

Let's imagine for a minute, though, that you pass the coding test and get an onsite interview. If you're not solid in that language, you can bet you wish you were as you face the white board, marker in hand, trying to answer a challenging problem posed to you by someone who's already made it across the divide and doesn't want to spend time with those who haven't done their homework. It's not enough to merely know the language. You need to know the esoteric elements and technical details of the language very well.

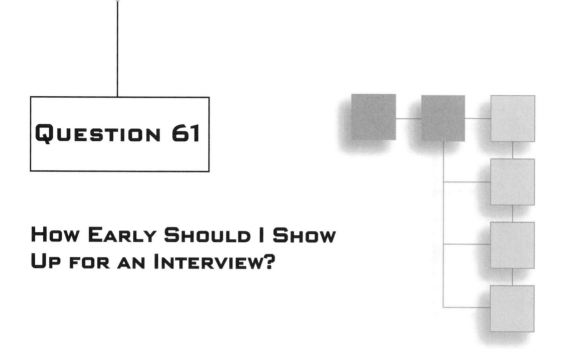

QUESTION 61

HOW EARLY SHOULD I SHOW UP FOR AN INTERVIEW?

Ian: This is another one of those things like what to wear, that some people stress over, even though it's not nearly the most important thing. (The most important thing about the interview is showing that you can help the company make a great game.) Arriving up to about 15 minutes early is fine; any more than that and you can expect to sit around waiting for a while. If you arrive too early and feel like it would be too awkward to walk in, feel free to sit in the parking lot composing yourself, or get out and take a short walk to relax (weather permitting).

Avoid being late, of course. The best defense against this is to know where you're going ahead of time; have a map with you, and preferably make the trip a day or two before the interview so you know where you're going. Also take along the phone number of the office you're visiting so you can call in case you do get lost (in this worst-case scenario, call as soon as you need help so that they know you're running late; it's better than showing up an hour late and making excuses after the fact).

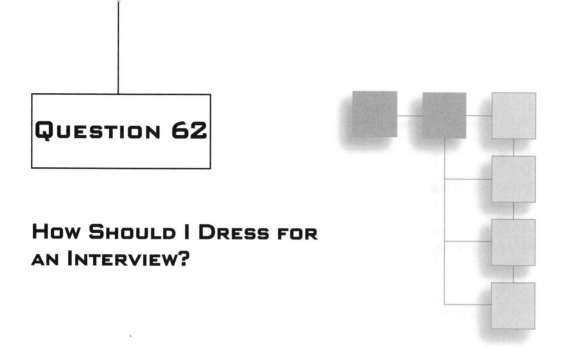

QUESTION 62

How Should I Dress for an Interview?

Ian: First-time interviewees often agonize over this, probably because it's much less scary than what happens in the actual interview, and it's something you can control. Here's the good news: Compared to related industries, the game industry is largely a meritocracy, and you will be hired (or not) based on whether the company thinks you're the best for the job . . . no matter what you're wearing.

That said, dress code at the vast majority of game companies is casual, so don't be surprised if your interviewer is wearing shorts, a T-shirt, and bare feet (in warmer climates, anyway). Coming to the interview in a suit and tie will likely get you gently teased, but it won't be the basis for a hire-or-don't-hire decision. "Business casual" dress is pretty safe. Casual (jeans, T-shirts) is probably okay. Ultra-casual (ripped clothing, lack of evidence of recent bathing) is probably not.

If you're the kind of person to stress about this, the easiest thing to do is ask about preferred dress when they contact you to set up an interview. Just say, "I understand this varies among companies, so how do you prefer people to dress for the interview?" No one will think any less of you. If you're so excited at getting the interview that you forget, it's not a problem to get in touch with that person later.

If you're curious about my own experience, for my first interview at a game company, I showed up in a suit and tie because I didn't know any better.

The hiring manager told me: "We're going to hire you, but if you ever show up dressed like that again, you're fired."

Ted Peterson (1993, Lead Game Designer, Disney Online Studios): For my first interview in games, I wore a suit. I told that to my first assistant, during the interview when I hired him. He was in a tux.

Monjoni Osso (2008, QA Lead and Game Design Lead, Paper Child Studios): I usually dress fairly casual for interviews, although with a bit of flair. Typical attire is an open long or short-sleeved button-down shirt, with a normal T-shirt under that, and a simple pair of blue jeans. I make sure to shave and be extremely clean before each interview, as well, as no one likes a smelly interviewee.

One thing I can definitely *not* recommend is wearing suits. At GDC 2008 I was looking for work, and I decided a neat getup would be a pinstripe suit that I had, along with a long sleeve gray button-down, with T-shirt worn underneath. The T-shirt had an image of Superman opening his shirt to reveal the famous S-shield. I had thought it would be a neat trick to, when asked, open up the button-down to reveal the T-shirt beneath (usually done when people asked why I was wearing a suit). This particular venture ended ... poorly. While I did get some great laughs and some opportunities to hand out my business card, I also got no e-mails back from interested parties!

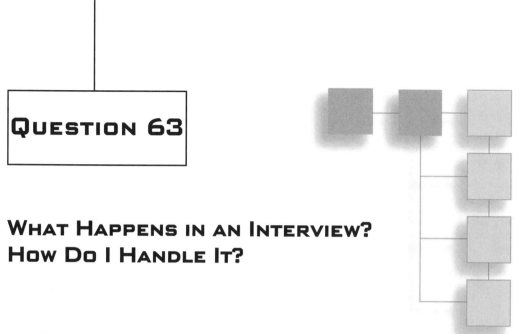

QUESTION 63

WHAT HAPPENS IN AN INTERVIEW?
HOW DO I HANDLE IT?

Ian: You know those old police shows, where the suspect is being given the "third degree" until they confess to murder? It's not exactly like that, but you might feel like it is. Even if the people interviewing you are incredibly nice, when you're applying for your dream job, you will probably feel a bit intimidated throughout. This feeling is normal.

Every company's interview process is different, but there are a few common threads. You may get a tour of the office. You'll meet with a lot of people, including your potential manager (or future boss), future co-workers within your department, and various lead developers or managers of other departments. You may meet people in a series of one-on-one grillings, or a single one-on-many interrogation where a panel of people fire off questions from all directions. These people will ask you questions, and you'll answer them. They will also typically ask if you have any questions of them, after they're done torturing you. You will also usually meet with someone in HR ("human resources") who will explain details like salary range and benefits of your position and important work policies; this person is not usually involved in the hiring decision, and is simply there to give you information and answer any logistical questions you might have, so you can relax during this part.

Duration varies wildly. I've been in some interviews where I just talked to a few people for 15 or 30 minutes each, and was out of there in an hour or two. Other interviews were half-day or all-day affairs, including a "casual" lunch with the team (not as casual as it appears, since you're still being interviewed during that time).

Overall, a company is trying to figure out three key things during the interview process:

- **Can you do the job?** That is, do you have the skills that will help them to make a great game? Can you hit the ground running on the current project, or will there be significant ramp-up time? Do your long-term career plans fit with the company's long-term hopes for someone in your position? (Not that many companies stay around that long, but we all like to pretend that our company will still be making games in 50 years. Humor us.) For many interviews, you are tested on your ability to solve problems live (for example, programmers might be asked to write some code on a whiteboard, or designers might be asked to create a simple system, a level, or some content).

- **Do you really want the job?** If they give you a job offer, will you turn it down? Or worse, will you take it, and then leave in a few months to take another offer? Do you really understand what you're getting yourself into?

- **Will you fit on the team?** Will you get along with your co-workers and generally make the space around you a great place to work, or are you a jerk who will make everyone in a 10-foot radius suddenly hate their jobs? Do you fit the company culture?

Your goal is to convince your interviewers that the answers to these three questions are all *Yes.* Consider asking your contact there (or a recruiter if you're using one) if there is a list of people you'll be meeting with. It gives you an opportunity to do some research on these people beforehand. And no matter what else you do, make sure you are familiar with the latest press and products from the company! Nothing sells inexperience quite like, "Oh, I haven't heard of that game series that you would have me working on."

One thing a lot of people stress about is what questions will be asked in an interview, and what are the right answers. The following is an excerpt from one of my blog posts called "The Interview Game" (http://teachingdesign.blogspot.com/2008/01/interview-game.html), which answers this specifically:

Ah, this is the heart of the matter, and the reason why I call this an interview "game." Because it *is* a game. For the company, the goal is to find the best candidate. For you, the goal is to get a job offer, *and* to figure out if this is an offer you'd accept. It's a turn-based game, where the interviewer asks a question and then you answer it. Here's the secret, though: The game is stacked in favor of the interviewee!

Here's why. For every question asked, the interviewer is giving away information about the company: its values, its culture, and the kinds of things it's looking for in a candidate. And they speak first, so you always have the information advantage. You win the game by deducing, in real-time, what each question really means. Then you can give an answer that works to your advantage, and you're ahead with each question *and* each answer.

Here are some examples of interview questions and what they really mean. You'll notice that I don't give any answers here. That's because there is no "right" answer; each answer you give is an expression of who you are. If I gave you answers, you'd be expressing who *I* am, but I'm not the one in that interview room. Also keep in mind that these are just examples. The trick here isn't to memorize these questions; it's to get used to the process of understanding what a question *really means* so that you're giving the interviewer the information they're looking for! As you can see, most questions are not 100% straightforward.

Question: How do you feel about working overtime?

Meaning: You will be working overtime. Do you think you'll enjoy this job so much that you won't mind when it takes control of your entire life from time to time? Most companies have at least some occasional "crunch," but since we're asking, you can expect to be doing mandatory overtime above your initial hopes/expectations.

What they really want to know: Are you passionate about this line of work, or are you looking for some cushy 40-hour-a-week desk job?

Question: Why did you leave your last employer? (Especially if this is not your first job in the game industry.)

Meaning: You left them. You'll probably leave us some day, too. Are you going to leave nicely, or are you going to be a jerk who causes problems for us?

What they really want to know: Right now you're on your way in so you'll act like you're our best friend. How will you treat us on the way out?

Worst possible answers: "I was fired for incompetence." (True perhaps, but suggests that the same thing will happen here. If you were fired and didn't quit, find a way to present this that makes it clear that any problems you had are in the past.) "I couldn't stand that company, the people sucked, the working conditions were terrible, I just couldn't stand it anymore." (Badmouthing a previous employer is a huge no-no. Aside from the implication that you'll be spreading bad PR about future employers down the road, the person interviewing you might have some friends they respect at that other company, and if it's your word against a personal friend, you are probably not going to be taken at your word.)

Question: What's your biggest weakness? (Variant: If I hire you, what will be my greatest regret after six months of working with you?)

Meaning: We know that no one's perfect, and that's okay. We just want to know that you're willing to become aware of your own imperfections, and that you can improve them or work around them.

What they really want to know: Are you capable of reflecting on your past experiences and finding your own faults? Also, can you take criticism well (you probably can if you spend time criticizing yourself)?

Worst possible answers: "My biggest weakness is that I'm totally incompetent and will single-handedly run your company into the ground." (Honest, perhaps, but doesn't tell them what they want to know.) "My biggest weakness is that I work too hard." (Total BS and we know it, and implies that you're unwilling to give yourself serious critique.) "I don't have any weaknesses." (Everyone has weaknesses, but if you're living in denial of real problems, how are you possibly going to accept the harsh realities of a project?)

Then there are the technical questions that vary by field. Some are straightforward tests of your ability; on the bright side, the more rigorous the testing, the more likely that your co-workers will be highly skilled as well. Sometimes you'll hear a question that sounds very strange unless you realize what it is they're *really* looking for; these curveballs are critical to showing that you can think critically about your chosen field. Some examples:

Design question: Pretend you're an architect. Design me a house.

Meaning: How do you approach a totally open-ended project?

Worst possible answers: Jump in and start drawing floor plans (shows that you're willing to design a game without doing any research ahead of time). Complain that you're not an architect and it's an unfair question (shows you're unwilling to learn something new, or stray outside your comfort zone, and you don't understand enough of game design to see the parallels with architecture).

QA question: Explain how to use a telephone. (Variant: Explain to a space alien who's never seen one.)

Meaning: How do you describe the steps to reproduce a simple bug to someone who's never seen it?

Worst possible answers: Complain that everyone already knows how to use one, so the question is pointless (shows that you don't understand enough about QA to see the parallel between explaining something obvious and explaining "obvious" repro steps for a bug). Be condescending or patronizing in your explanation (implies you'll treat programmers the same way if they can't follow your written repro steps).

Programming question: Explain the concept of class inheritance in terms that my technophobic grandmother could understand.

Meaning: Communication skills are important for programmers, particularly being able to explain technical ideas to nontechnical people (such as designers, artists, and producers).

Worst possible answers: Give an explanation right out of your Computer Science textbook (shows that you only know how to communicate with other programmers). Say that you don't know what class inheritance is (proves you were sleeping through your core curriculum). Say that it's impossible to explain such a technical thing to someone who has no programming experience, so it's an unfair question (shows not only that you can't communicate with non-technical people, but you're not even going to try).

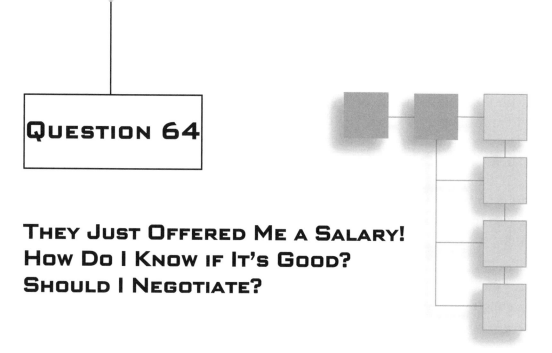

QUESTION 64

THEY JUST OFFERED ME A SALARY! HOW DO I KNOW IF IT'S GOOD? SHOULD I NEGOTIATE?

Brenda: First of all, never, *ever* agree to what they offered right there on the phone, even if it sounds like much more than you were hoping for. You always want time to think it over (even if it turns out you don't actually need that time). HR people may try to rush an answer out of you by saying that the offer is good only for a set amount of time or that they need to have an answer immediately for some particular reason. Your best defense is a prepared offense. "Thank you. I'm going to think that over and get back to you shortly." If they say they were hoping for an answer immediately, tell them that you promise to get back to them as close to "immediately" as you can, but that you do need some time. It's best if you've researched salary ahead of time so that you don't have to spend time figuring it out shortly after you've received your offer. *Game Developer Magazine* publishes yearly salary surveys that take into account both newbies and veteran salaries. That's a good place to start. If you're fortunate to know someone in the industry, feel free to ask them what they think your starting salary should be. That information should let you know whether you're at least in the right ballpark. Next, know that what they're offering you is what they are hoping you accept. They are almost always willing to go higher than that. So, if they say, "We're offering you $55K," you could likely push to $58 or $59K without too much trouble. Odds are, they will meet you somewhere in the middle. So, in the previous scenario, if I were hoping to get $58K, I might push to $65K and say simply, "I was hoping to get closer to $65. Could we perhaps meet somewhere in the middle?" The recruiter will likely need to check back with the powers that be before confirming or denying the amount. The reason that this matters is that every dollar up you are, it's a dollar you don't have to fight for in raises. You literally are shaving a year off your salary trajectory. Be careful not to go too nuts in asking for more. Sometimes, they will come back and say, "$55 is all we can do. It is what we budgeted for the role." If you want the gig, take it. It's not hip to push back and forth, particularly when you are trying to break in. If you're a rock star with a résumé a mile long, that's another thing entirely.

Ian: First of all, congratulations! If this is your first job offer in the industry, that is a huge milestone. Most people face a lot of rejections before that first offer, so getting the offer is, at least emotionally, a nice way to feel validated.

Next, a couple of things you should know so you're prepared. When people refer to a "salary" that means you get paid the same amount no matter how many hours you work, as opposed to an hourly wage, where you get paid by the hour rather than by the week/month/year. Being salaried is also sometimes referred to as being "exempt" because your company does not legally have to pay you extra for overtime hours. Although being salaried sounds like a status symbol to anyone who has played *Monopoly* and passed Go, really it is nothing to get all that excited about—it just means the company has the right to extract as much labor from you as it possibly can for one flat rate. Keep this in your mind so you aren't so impressed by the word "salary" that you miss the other details.

Also, salary that is quoted with a "K" after it means that many thousand dollars (even though the word "thousand" does not contain the letter "K"—blame the metric system). However, just to confuse you, if you are offered a "401(k)" that does *not* mean your salary is $401,000. The 401(k) is a reference to the U.S. tax code section that describes a certain type of retirement plan, and most companies have something like this, so it's not that special. The actual salary is what you should pay more attention to.

At this point, you might be a little bit afraid that if you do anything other than say, "Yes, I'll take it," the company will decide it's too much hassle and you'll lose your one chance to break in. This is actually the *last* thing you need to worry about. The company has already undoubtedly conducted a long, expensive hiring search, and they've determined that you are the best fit for the job. They do *not* want the best candidate to walk away just after they've finally found you. Since you've been given an offer, you are in a rare position of power (one that, incidentally, evaporates as soon as you say "yes, I'll take it"). If you're talking to some random HR person and not a developer, even better—the *last* thing this person wants to do is report to the hiring manager that they blew the negotiations and you walked. So do what you can in that tiny window of opportunity.

If you are uncomfortable naming a specific number as Brenda suggests (some people have a hard time placing a numeric value on their work), another tactic is to simply say "Hmm... you can't go any higher than that?" and see what they say. If the answer is no, at least you know it's non-negotiable. But most of the time, the person you're talking to is *expecting* to negotiate, and this question immediately transitions to wheeling-and-dealing mode, where you want to be. Even if the person calling you is from HR, they might not need to check with anyone to start negotiations with you; they might have been given a starting salary and an acceptable range from the Powers That Be, so be prepared to launch into salary discussions right away if that happens.

One note about salary ranges: The company might have a desired range, and you probably have your own range. It is said that whoever first names a number in the negotiations, loses; and there is some truth to that. If asked for your desired salary (or range), first see if you can sidestep the question: "Well, what is the range your company typically offers for this position?" and then work from there. But if you *have* given a desired salary range and they make an offer right in the middle of that range, they are giving you a reasonable offer based on the information you've provided; having a number in the middle of a range you gave them is your signal to stop negotiating on price. It's also worth saying that salary negotiations should happen *after* you receive a job offer, not before. If you're asked about desired salary during the interview, dodge the question as best you can. For example, "I have every confidence in you to make a competitive offer." Or "Let's talk about that after we've both decided there is a good fit here."

I'll close with a few traps that you should be aware of:

- **"It's a low base salary, but we make it up with higher-than-average annual raises."** First of all, this is just saying that you'll get money later rather than now, for no good reason. Second, a verbal promise of future raises over the phone is non-binding, and it's anyone's guess whether the supposed raises will ever materialize. Don't be surprised if at the end of the year, you hear about how it's been such a tough year for the company and they can't afford the big raises or bonuses that they'd like to hand out ...

- **"It's a low base salary, but some people here get a lot more with bonuses and royalties for the projects they worked on."** Statistically, about 90% of game projects fail to turn a profit at all (you can bet you'll get a percentage of *profit*, not *revenue*, meaning you only make money if the company does), and less than 5% ever earn enough to bring in royalties if the developer received an advance from a publisher. Although you might be lucky enough to work on a massive hit that generates substantial cash for the entire team, realize that it is like buying a lottery ticket. The odds are stacked against you, and it is very likely you'll see nothing at all, no matter how many success stories at the company are paraded around in front of you. Also, if you are working on a really large team, even a decent-sized royalty will be so diluted that your share will be tiny ... especially if junior-level employees or recent hires like you get a smaller share than those with seniority.

- **"It's a low base salary, but we make it up with a better benefits package."** Sometimes there *is* something to this—benefits like health insurance, dental, and 401(k) might add up to a substantial amount of cash savings compared to if you had to buy them yourself—so ask for details. Add up the cash value of the benefits (you might have to take some guesses here) and see if that makes your total compensation package more reasonable. However, beware—some "benefits" like free catered meals *sound* great in theory, but are really designed to maximize the number of hours you're in the office each day. These benefits should be considered as overtime pay, *not* as a base salary boost.

- **"We need an answer right away."** No, they really don't. They just spent how many months in a job search only to mysteriously run out of time now? Unlikely. This is a pressure tactic that should be a huge red flag; probably, their offer is not very competitive and they know it, and they're hoping you'll answer before you have time to do your research. Say anything you can to buy time, as Brenda suggests. Another line of defense against this is to research expected salary/benefits *before* you get an offer, so you immediately know if you're getting low-balled. Be prepared to negotiate on the spot if you have to. If they refuse to give you more time, ask yourself if that's the kind of company you want to work for, if they value you so little at the one time when you have any kind of power.

- **"We offer a competitive base salary."** Maybe the salary figure seems pretty good. Remember that salary is only one aspect of your overall job. See Question 67 for other things to consider.

QUESTION 65

DO INTERVIEWEES EVER SAY DUMB THINGS?

Brenda: One of my favorite times of the interview process is "the lunch." It's when we take the candidate out to lunch along with those individuals with whom he or she might be working. The atmosphere of the lunch is laid back and not only allows the whole team a chance to interact with the person, but it gives us a chance to see them with their proverbial guard down. My favorite story of all time involves a man whom I've come to know as "The Dictator." During a lunch interview, one of the artists casually asked how he would have run things if he were in charge. "Like a dictator," he said. "So that I could ensure things would get done the way that I wanted them to." I was offered and took the job he didn't get. His interview, for all intents and purposes, ended there.

I decided to poll some of my game development friends on Twitter. Not surprisingly, the consensus is, "Yes, interviewees do say dumb things." Of course, a whole book could be also filled with stupid things interview*ers* say, but that's another matter.

- @_nits: "Nobody uses C anymore."
- @jeevesmeister: "'You're so hot' to a recruiter will never get old in my book."
- @crsteinb: "Wouldn't talk about games they liked, or things they were interested in. You need experiences in this industry to draw from."
- @siawnhy: "When asked what game he'd make with 30mil and free reign, he says, 'I've read NDAs before, so I know you could steal my idea.'"

- @stuartjeff: "When asked what sort of games he plays: 'I only play the big game … [dramatic pause] programming.' Okay, thanks for your time."

- @wknoxwalker: "I didn't need a degree but the industry wouldn't recognize my talent without one."

- @Domino_EQ2: "Two recent graduates who studied together at college interviewed separately, and both tried to throw the other under the bus."

- @EmberDione: "A game design interviewee: 'I don't have time to play games right now.' In response to 'What games are you currently playing?'"

- @Dclowery: "Genre_Leading_Game_01 is a terrible game and I don't understand why anyone likes it."

- @mzamara: "Me: 'So, are you familiar with our games?' Them: 'No, I don't really like social games.'"

- @shift9: "When interviewing for a social game gig: 'Oh, I don't play those types of games. They're terrible. I play real games.'"

- @jetsers: "'I'm hard core.' You may as well give up there if you tell me that."

- @jesawyer: "After about six to eight months on a project, I kind of just get bored with it and want to work on something else."

- @JohnComes: "Q: What can you do for us? A: Well, nothing, you guys seem to have thought of everything I would have."

- @decapodstudios: "'My hobby is throwing knives' … seconds of silence … Okay, we'll get in touch."

- @robinyang: "How many of your best designers, lead designers, or even creative directors have been trained to design games? I bet the answer is none. I have training and experience. I am one of the very few people in the nation who do!"

- @deldesigner: "Regarding second meetings—no treating them like a second date. No 'I thought our ideas really clicked' or sycophantic bull."

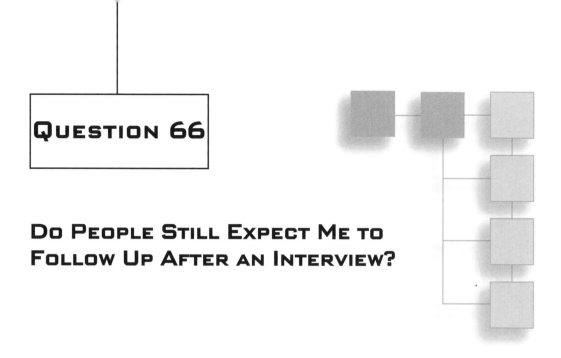

QUESTION 66

DO PEOPLE STILL EXPECT ME TO FOLLOW UP AFTER AN INTERVIEW?

Brenda: Absolutely. A quick follow-up e-mail to those you interviewed with is always appropriate.

> "Thanks so much for the opportunity to interview with you for the position of [x]. It was great to learn about [company name or project if applicable]. I look forward to hearing from you at your earliest convenience and, in the meantime, feel free to contact me should you require further information or have additional questions."

That's a bit on the dry side for many, but it's a safe professional bet. Never follow up with a message to a personal account—Facebook or personal e-mail. Also, don't thank people via Twitter. That's their personal space, and unless they specifically tell you to ping them on Twitter, don't.

After the first thank-you message, it's okay to ping the HR person or recruiter every couple of weeks, but don't do it more than that unless they ask you to check back. Those who follow up too aggressively rub people the wrong way.

Ian: Just to be clear, write your own follow-up email, don't just quote Brenda's example or any others you find word for word. You don't think the person you're sending it to might have read this book or seen identical wordings from others?

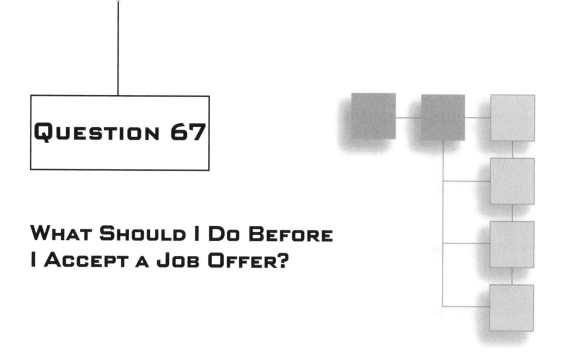

QUESTION 67

WHAT SHOULD I DO BEFORE I ACCEPT A JOB OFFER?

Ian: First, be sure you want the job. During the interview, you probably met a bunch of people, were asked a lot of pointed questions, and saw the office space where you'll be working. Close your eyes and picture yourself there; is this the kind of place where you think you'd like to spend the majority of your waking hours for at least the next year, if not 10? Accepting a job is like accepting a new romantic partner into your life: Unless you're completely desperate, a bad relationship is worse than none at all. If you have any people you know and trust who used to work at that company, ask them what it's like, especially the best and worst parts; it's hard to get a perfect feel for a place from one short interview.

Second, make sure you receive an official offer (usually sent in a letter or e-mail) that details exactly what is being offered to you, including base salary, benefits, and anything else that's part of the offer, and also including what exactly are the expectations of you. Get a copy of the employment contract and any other paperwork they'll have you sign, if you can, and look it over (see Questions 68 and 69).

Then there are the practical aspects. If the job is in a new city, will you have to pay to move, or will the company pay for relocation (or will *you* pay up front, then get reimbursed)? Can you afford the up-front cost of moving in the first place? If not, let the company know—if they're willing to hire you, they may be willing to give you a short-term loan and take it back out of your first few paychecks, or something of that nature.

Also consider your living expenses, versus base salary and benefits; can you afford to work there and still keep your current standard of living, or would you need to downgrade, or do you have obligations that require a certain minimum salary? Importantly, "base salary" must be taken in context with the cost of living; it's harder to live off $50,000 in a high-cost area like New York than it is to live on half of that in a low-cost area like South Dakota. Use an online "cost of living calculator" to convert the salary to an area you're familiar with so you can compare (actually, use several cost of living calculators since they'll all give slightly different numbers, and use that as a ballpark estimate).

Consider if the salary is fair. Each year, *Game Developer Magazine* sends out a salary survey, giving the average salary based on position, experience, geographic location, and other variables. Although the numbers tend to run a little higher than reality (a lot of people inflate their salary in the vain hope that they can show the report to their boss and angle for a raise), they will at least tell you if what you're being offered is competitive, or a lowball. Even if you can afford an obnoxiously low salary, ask yourself if you shouldn't earn what you're worth if you are given an offer that seems lower than it should be.

However, don't look at salary alone. Benefits (particularly financial ones like retirement plans and subsidized health insurance) can add a lot of dollars in your pocket indirectly, so be sure to count that. Many companies offer other benefits that sound like they just improve your quality of life: free gym passes, free or discounted games, and so on. Be careful: Some of these "benefits" are specifically designed to keep you working in the office as long as possible, and could signal the expectation of long "crunch" periods that will take you away from your home and your family. Although there is nothing implicitly wrong with free snacks and drinks in the lunch room, free catered meals, a dedicated gaming library, free at-your-desk massages on demand, a workout room on site, and so on, having many of these things is a red flag that should prompt further investigation and caution on your part (see Question 82).

Here's the good news: With a job offer in hand, the company has already said that you were the best person they could find for the position. This puts you in a position of power when negotiating. If the offer made to you is not acceptable, you can make a counteroffer, especially if you have a good reason beyond greed.

Naturally, if you've been lucky enough to have several interviews recently, you may be waiting to hear the results of others. If the company that is extending the offer isn't your first choice, kindly ask when they need to hear back (if they don't outright tell you when handing you the offer). Then contact the company (or companies) you'd prefer to work for, and ask them nicely when you can expect to hear back. If the two dates aren't in the same range and you can't negotiate with either one, you've got a tough choice to make. Whatever you do, don't let either company know that you're waiting to hear back on another offer; you may as well admit they're not your first choice, and companies have been known to rescind offers so you don't want to blow your chance now.

If you do accept the job, be nice and contact any other companies that you've applied to and let them know to remove you from their hiring pool. This is a courtesy, so be courteous; Remember that these other companies may be future employers, and you should treat them as such.

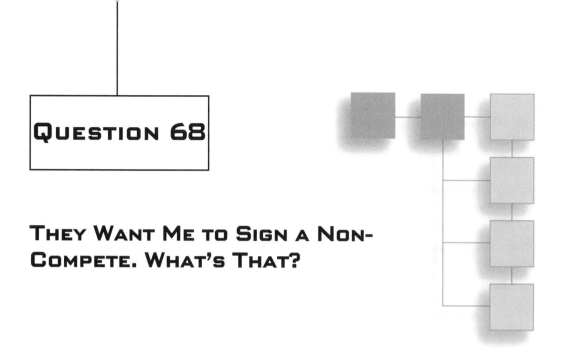

Question 68

They Want Me to Sign a Non-Compete. What's That?

Ian: It's a potentially dangerous document that you should look over very, very carefully before signing. Do not confuse a non-disclosure agreement (NDA), which is standard and generally harmless, with a non-compete agreement, which tends to be far more restrictive in the kinds of activities you can do professionally.

At its heart, a non-compete provides some protection for your employer should you decide to use the skills you've learned on the job to create a product that competes with theirs. If you work at a company that makes Facebook games, for example, your boss might not be too pleased if you made your own Facebook game on your own time that competed with the company's main product. Your employer also wouldn't be particularly happy if you left to work at a competitor, especially if you convinced half of your co-workers to follow you. These are the kinds of situations that a non-compete is (very reasonably) trying to prevent.

Unfortunately, some non-competes fail to draw the line between malicious abuse and standard industry practice. A non-compete might, for example, restrict you from working as a game developer for any competitor at all, for the time that you work there plus two years (the extra time is added on so that you can't immediately release a competing game the day after you leave). In practice, such an agreement would effectively mean that you can't work in the game industry at all for two years after leaving the company. How were you planning to pay the bills, in that case? Even if not intentional, some non-competes fail to clearly define what counts as "competition" (is it all games, or just those within a certain genre or platform?), leading to language that may end up being more restrictive than it first appears.

Thankfully, some non-competes are so unfair that they are legally unenforceable, so if you do accidentally sign your life away, you may have some measure of protection. However, it is best not to tempt fate on this. Read carefully, and consider hiring an attorney to look it over if you are not sure or do not understand it completely. And while it's your life and your choice, I would not recommend signing a document that puts you at significant risk for extended unemployment.

There is a catch with this, of course. Suppose you apply for a job, go through the interview process, receive an offer, take the job, move across the country. . . and then on your first day, you have to fill out some paperwork, and here's this non-compete staring you in the face that is now a condition of your employment. Then what do you do? If you don't sign it, you're out of work, and you've got less money after paying for moving expenses, so you would appear to be stuck.

The best defense against that situation is to find out ahead of time. When you formally accept a job offer, ask if they can mail/fax/e-mail you all of the paperwork for your first day on the job, so you can at least get a heads-up if there's any suspicious language in the contract, before you move. At the very least, you can come right out and ask if you'll need to sign a non-compete or similar form.

Brenda: Know the laws and use your pen. In some states, including California, non-competes are illegal except in very limited circumstances. I have also known people to cross off offending phrases, initial next to them before signing and ask for a copy. The HR person didn't bat an eye. As Ian points out, when in doubt, always consult a lawyer. It is common for employers to not mention non-competes until the first day on the job. As Ian notes, you should most certainly ask about it after you have received a written offer.

QUESTION 69

THEY WANT ME TO SIGN AN NDA. WHAT'S THAT?

Ian: NDA stands for *non-disclosure agreement*, and it is probably the one document you will sign more than any other in your game development career. You'll almost certainly be signing one at every job that you accept. You may have to sign one at an interview, if the company is sufficiently paranoid. Developers who are working at startups may ask you to sign an NDA just to talk to them about their project at all, even if it's just to beta test the thing. In fact, you can usually get a sense of how long someone has been in the industry by asking how many NDAs they've signed: If they have lost count, they are an industry veteran; if they stopped counting so long ago that they don't even *remember* when they lost count, they've been doing this for longer than you've been alive.

The purpose of an NDA is to protect the company in the event that you say something stupid. It is, in essence, an agreement that you may be exposed to information that is confidential to the company and that may cause real damage if that information is leaked (for example, talking about an innovative game mechanic that might be implemented by the competition, or mentioning a product that hasn't been officially announced yet). By signing the NDA, you agree that you won't do that, and that you'll take reasonable steps to protect the information (such as, um, not tweeting or blogging about it as soon as you leave the office), and that if you're stupid enough to do this anyway, the company can sue your pants off.

By all means, read everything before you sign it. But NDAs are mostly harmless, and part of the normal course of doing business with game companies.

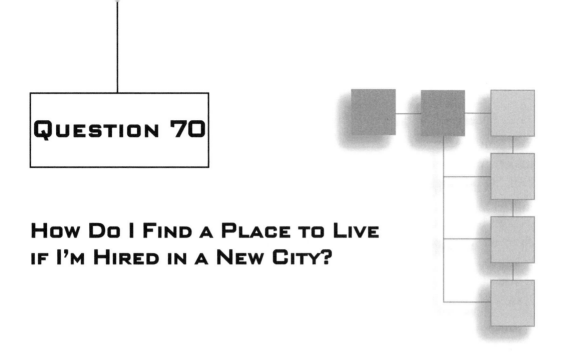

QUESTION 70

HOW DO I FIND A PLACE TO LIVE IF I'M HIRED IN A NEW CITY?

Ian: Every city is different, but there are a few general strategies. The easiest place to start is by asking the company that hired you; everyone there had to find a place to live at some point, so most of them should be able to give you pointers on finding a place. One place that I was hired at even had someone on the development team who'd been looking for a roommate to split the rent, so I was able to get a short-term place to live from the first day, giving me time to find another more permanent place—and I never would have known if I didn't ask. Your new co-workers also know the area and can recommend what neighborhoods to seek out or avoid. Some companies may even offer to cover some of your relocation expenses, or they may have special deals with local realtors.

If you're in a position where you can move before your work officially starts, assuming you have some spare cash on hand, you can stay in a hotel for a few nights and spend the days scouting out neighborhoods and home-hunting. This method can work well in locations where housing is relatively easy to find. Sometimes this is covered in the relocation benefit; you can always ask.

For some cities where housing is difficult to find, you may need to start your search earlier if possible. When I moved to Boston in the year 2001, it generally took about a month to find a decent apartment, and that was if you used a realtor and paid a fee that would have been considered robbery anywhere else. When I moved to Tucson five years before that, you could get a decent apartment in a week without any outside help. If you're not sure, ask anyone at the company and they should be able to tell you the general housing situation. They all had to figure this out, after all.

You can search for apartments online (there are many websites for this; for major metropolitan areas, housingmaps.com is a useful resource that pulls housing postings from craigslist) and usually have a place ready to go before you move. The danger here is that you are signing a lease, sight unseen, so it may not exactly be the luxurious space you were hoping for. If you do this, try to get a short lease so that you can exit quickly if you end up living in a rat hole. Keep in mind that short-term leases tend to be marginally more expensive per month, so if you absolutely love the place you're staying, you can negotiate a longer-term lease to lower your rent.

As with many things, money can be traded off for time if that is an option. If you're willing to pay more, generally speaking, you can get a nicer place on short notice. If you're short on cash, it may take longer to find a place that meets your needs. Do your best to plan accordingly.

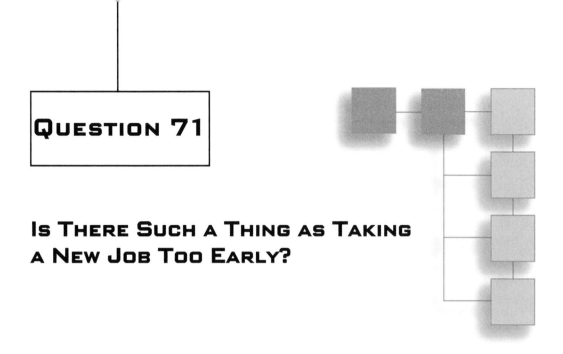

QUESTION 71

IS THERE SUCH A THING AS TAKING A NEW JOB TOO EARLY?

Brenda: Yes. There are a couple rules I've shared with a great many people, and I consider them so important that I have literally lived my career around them or learned them through a false step I wished I had not made.

Rule 1: Never leave until the game ships. There is a general unspoken rule in the industry that, barring some kind of horrific situation, you will stay in the job until the game ships. This becomes more and more important the higher your rank is. Trying to replace a lead mid-project is a true nightmare, and even though your new employer might be thrilled you're able to join, future employers will think twice when they see you've abandoned ship. (For the record, I have never abandoned a game in development.)

Rule 2: Only make "+1" moves. So, if you're a PC RPG designer, becoming a lead PC RPG designer is a possible move. Becoming a lead designer on an action-adventure RPG for a console is a +2 move (+1 for lead and +1 for the new platform). I've seen all kinds of situations where people jump into situations that are offered to them only to get in way over their heads. (For the record, I made a +3 move once. You don't want to do that.)

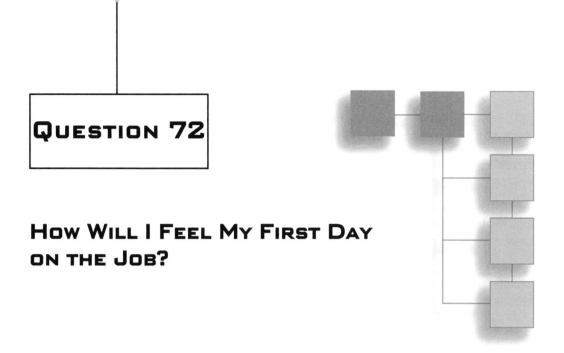

QUESTION 72

HOW WILL I FEEL MY FIRST DAY ON THE JOB?

Ian: I suppose everyone is different, but if you're anything like me, you'll probably feel equal parts excited and terrified. You might be elated that you finally "made it" and that you're now working at your "dream job." You may be star struck at all the incredibly awesome and talented people you'll be working with, who now count you as one of their peers. You'll be afraid of doing something stupid, making people suddenly regret that they hired you. You'll worry that you're not good enough, and that any day now, someone will look at your work and declare you the fraud that you are secretly afraid you are. These feelings are all normal and natural, and will mostly fade with time, as you get up to speed on whatever the current project is.

At the same time, you may be surprised at the amount of paperwork and ramping up you need to do before you start any "real" work. You'll probably sign an endless blur of forms: employment agreement, NDA, benefits enrollment. You'll be presented with a lot of reading: benefits explanations, company policy manual, perhaps a style guide for your department. You may need to set up your workspace, install software on your computer, or work with IT to get yourself on the company's intranet and e-mail systems. This time doesn't even account for getting yourself familiar with the right project files and servers and so on. This may be a massive ramp if you're a coder. More than one company I've worked for did not even have a computer ready for me on the day I started; it always took a few days for them to get me set up! On the bright side, this removes some of the pressure; for an entry-level position, no one expects you to perform miracles on your first day on the job. Use the time to learn about the company culture, and generally the way things are done there.

Brenda: No matter how long you've been in the industry or how many jobs you've held, odds are that you'll feel overwhelmed that first day. You might even feel kind of ignored if your lead is very busy and crunching to get something done, or you might feel buried if he or she dumps a ton of stuff on you. If you were hired in as lead, you may find yourself with a bunch of direct reports who have been desperately awaiting your arrival and who require both work to do and have lots of complaints about how things are currently being done. The feeling may come—and it may come strongly—that you are way underqualified for the job or that you have a shocking amount to learn. This is particularly true if you are transitioning between spaces (AAA to social games, for instance) or have joined a company with lots of proprietary tech. In moments where I have felt such foreboding feelings, I have asked myself two questions: "Do I know what I am doing right this minute?" The answer is almost always yes. It's the horizon that terrifies us. The second question I ask is, "If I don't know, do I know someone who does?" The answer to that is *always* yes. These questions stave off a great deal of angst.

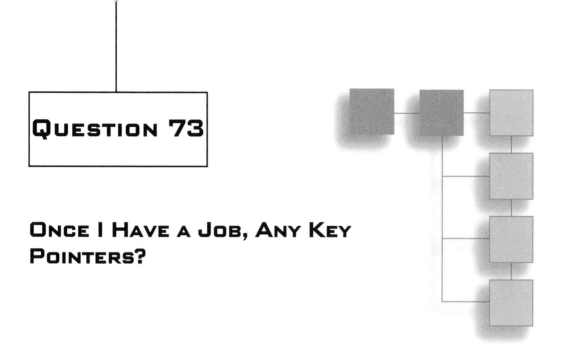

QUESTION 73

ONCE I HAVE A JOB, ANY KEY POINTERS?

Ian: When you first start out, do the best work you can; first impressions count for a lot. What can you do to be the most effective? First, do anything you're told to do. Second, find as much background material on the current project and the company as you can, and familiarize yourself. If there are existing design documents for the project you were hired in, read them, and also research similar games in the same genre. If the company has "post-mortems" of previous projects available, read those to get a sense of the problems that keep recurring, so you know what to expect moving forward. If the company is using software or tools you haven't seen before, play around with them a bit in a safe environment to get up to speed. Basically, do whatever you can to ramp up quickly so you can become productive.

The flip side to this is to avoid draining away the productivity of others. You will undoubtedly run into things you don't know or don't understand. Avoid the temptation to run to a senior or lead every five minutes; these other people are probably happy to help you, but remember that they have their own tasks to complete, and they make no progress while they talk to you. Try writing down your questions, saving them up, and then asking them in a batch every now and then. This is particularly important for coders whose work suffers with constant context switching.

Brenda: Resist the temptation to chime in on everything. No one likes the newbie who has a great idea on how to change everything or make everything better.

In fact, these people are often hated. Your first few months on the job are an important time for you to do what you were hired to do, to learn and to absorb the company culture. Another thing I have seen new game devs do is ask too few questions or provide 150% when they were merely asked for 100%. The best design, for instance, is not always the best design within the given constraints. So, while your idea might be awesome, it might also take 1.5 times as long as the project has allotted for its development. Resist the urge to pad designs with creativity. New devs are also frequently eager to quote short time estimates to impress their bosses. Make sure your estimates are accurate. You will either be known as "The Optimist" or "The One Who's Always Late," neither of which is appealing.

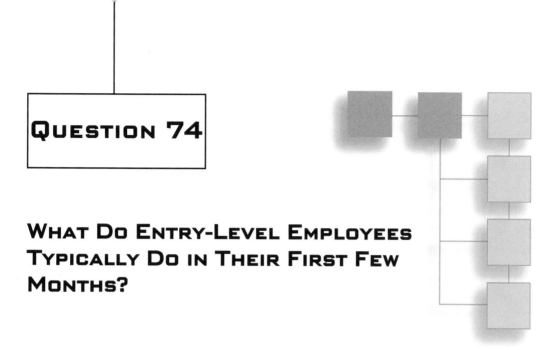

QUESTION 74

WHAT DO ENTRY-LEVEL EMPLOYEES TYPICALLY DO IN THEIR FIRST FEW MONTHS?

Brenda: It greatly depends on the company and the space that you're in (for example, social or console). Your first day will be the same most anywhere. You will fill out hordes of HR forms, get your computer rolling, and get access to the data you need. The remainder of the first week will likely be spent getting up to speed on this information and the product and waiting for all the information you're taking in to gel in your head. The following week, you will likely begin your assigned tasks in earnest, which they might not have told you about. For a designer or a coder, it's likely a system you'll be working on. For an artist, you will be assigned a task in the pipeline commensurate with your abilities. Level designers will be assigned an area or a task in an already existing level. Naturally, all this depends on the level at which you were brought onto the project and the project's lead, who may have specific "fires" she needs you to address. Another interesting thought is the inclusion of "first few months" in this question. In that time, one could ship an iPhone title or a Facebook game. With a console game, three months is about 1/8th of the dev cycle or less.

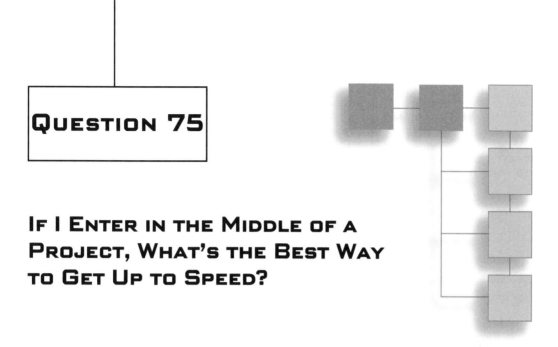

QUESTION 75

IF I ENTER IN THE MIDDLE OF A PROJECT, WHAT'S THE BEST WAY TO GET UP TO SPEED?

Ian: In the early phase of a project, a company can often get by with a small team of senior people throwing together pitch documents and quick-and-dirty prototypes. Once the project ramps up, they need more hands on deck, and that's the time the company goes on a hiring binge. Into this sudden rush when they need people getting work done now, you get hired. For many entry-level positions or companies with live products, this is the norm.

The first thing you should do is anything you're told to do. If you are given specific tasks to complete, get those done first, as your top priority. However, game development isn't like school—it is not a cycle of getting assignments, turning them in, and getting more assignments—and you will quickly find that others expect you to find your own ways of contributing when you run out of tasks on your official to-do list.

Early on, you can find out where the project documentation is and read it. If you're a programmer, see if there's a technical design document that describes the various systems, so you can understand how your code fits into the big picture. If the company is using a game engine or other coding tools, familiarize yourself with those tools, either by creating small sample projects or otherwise playing around with them to get a feel for the capabilities of your tools (provided your lead encourages you to, of course). Also, see if there's a coding style they follow, or some other guidelines for the preferred process of writing code. If you're an artist, look for an art bible, art style guide, pipeline documentation, or anything else that describes how art is made and what to do with it when the work is completed. If you're a game designer, read all of the design documents, especially those that pertain directly to the areas you'll be working in. Be sure to check that any documents you read are up to date, first; design docs in particular go out of date quickly, especially on live or highly iterative projects where changes happen live. Also familiarize yourself with other games in the same genre, if you are not already intimately familiar with the kind of game you're working on.

If the company has completed projects before, see if there are any "post-mortem" documents from those projects (that is, documentation of what went right and wrong on previous projects, written after the fact). Look for patterns; if you see the same difficulties cropping up on nearly every project, be forewarned that those are the challenges you will likely be facing later.

If you are given enough work to do that you don't have time during the work day to do all of this background reading/research, try to spend a couple of hours doing it after work, at least for the first few weeks or so. You'll already have a lot of extra energy from the excitement of a new job, and you can ramp up a lot faster if you can figure out where the team and the project are going.

As a general principle, try to do as much as you can on your own, and save up any questions you have so you can get them out of the way at once (it helps to write them down). While everyone on your team wants you to succeed and contribute, they are busy with their own contributions, and interrupting someone else's workflow every five minutes with yet another question will only succeed in stopping them from being productive.

It's also important to remember that your lead may have specific plans for you. Coming in with your own plans may work against this.

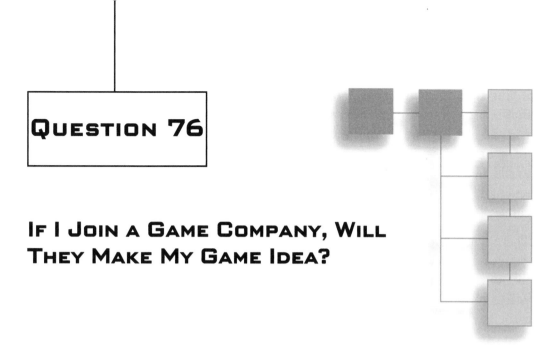

QUESTION 76

IF I JOIN A GAME COMPANY, WILL THEY MAKE MY GAME IDEA?

Ian: Ha ha ha... umm, no. At least, not in the way that you're hoping.

First, as mentioned elsewhere in this book, *everyone* on the development team has at least one "great idea" for a game. Do the math: dozens, maybe hundreds, of people on a team, but they can only work on one idea at a time, which means statistically, it'll be a while before they get to yours. More than that, though, is the funding issue: Who pays for the development team to make a game in the first place? Usually, it is an outside entity such as a publisher, and they are requesting you to make *their* games, not yours. They are paying you, after all, so this is only fair. If you want a development team to make your idea, then *you* pay them.

Okay, so you don't have millions of dollars lying around. What *can* you do? Happily, a lot of things, depending on what you're willing to compromise.

If you just want to have some creative influence on a game—that is, you'd like to have *some* of your ideas make it into a final game, something where you can point at the game and say, "Hey, look at that piece right there, that was my idea"—if you are a game designer, this will happen (to a greater or lesser degree) on every project you work on. If you aren't a game designer, on most teams, you are still free to talk to the designers and make suggestions (assuming you're nice about it and not overly pushy). If your ideas have merit, some of them may make it into the game in some form or other.

If you have this "high vision" for an original game idea that you want to make, that is a little bit harder. The fastest, easiest way to get this done is to go make it yourself, on your own time, with your own skills. If you lack some of the skills, learn new ones—it'll make you a better professional developer, anyway. If it would take too long to make your grand vision because it's a huge game, try scaling it down and challenging yourself to get the main idea across in a smaller game.

There is a slower, longer way to get your game made. Work on other people's games within the industry, and do an outstanding job making them. Keep doing this until you have reached a Creative Director level (this may take 20 or 30 years, most of your entire career). When your name is well known and associated with greatness, you *may* be given the opportunity to pitch your own project. *Once.* If the game isn't a major hit, you'll probably not get another chance. (An alternate slow, long way to get your game made is to work hard, make more money than you spend, aggressively save the rest, and when you have enough money put together, start your own company and finance your own game.)

Does that mean that it *never* happens that developers are allowed to pitch their own game ideas internally? Actually, some companies do allow this, and a few even encourage it. And yes, every now and then a game idea that comes from a budding developer picks up momentum and gets the green light. But this is the extremely rare exception, not the rule, so don't count on it. Look on the bright side: Your idea probably isn't as great as you think it is, anyway, and wouldn't it be embarrassing to have your employer lose millions of dollars by taking a risk on you that didn't work out?

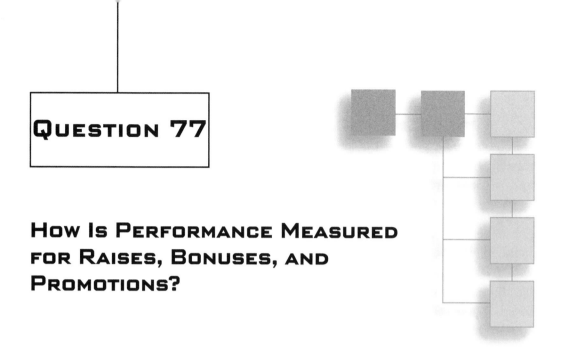

QUESTION 77

HOW IS PERFORMANCE MEASURED FOR RAISES, BONUSES, AND PROMOTIONS?

Brenda: The new game industry trend seems to be laying people off after a product, so it doesn't much matter how great your work is. For live games, there may be a bit more stability since more people are typically required after the product ships to support it and its extended features. In my time in the industry, I have seen performance measured in a variety of ways. The most traditional method is the yearly meeting with the powers that be to assess your work, determine your raise, establish some goals, and go forward from there. Some companies, including two I worked for in the last five years, did these appraisals quarterly with raises scheduled yearly. Oddly enough, the biggest raises don't come from promotions within—they come from swapping companies. Every veteran knows it. Mind you, in the early going, leaving one company for another too regularly is likely to have an adverse effect on you. Another method for appraisals is the "survey the co-workers" method. So, each of your co-workers is asked to assess your performance, and then your boss delivers you the results. This can often be phenomenally wonderful or phenomenally crushing, depending on the person, the company, and the co-workers.

Bonuses in the game industry are the stuff of legend. One of my dearest friends has been the recipient of multiple six-figure bonuses. I have received just one in all of my career—somewhere back in the 1980s, I received a Christmas bonus of one week's pay (but the company did give me 18 years of employment, so don't feel bad for me). Traditionally, bonuses are paid on ship (that is, when the game is released), but don't expect one. So much goes into determining whether bonuses are received or not that one should ever take them for granted.

Ian: Your main goal in the game industry is not to perform well so you get a raise, it's to ship a game that's good enough that the entire studio isn't closed and laid off. And even with a hit game, there are no guarantees on that front. With such low levels of job security, getting a bonus is not guaranteed.

Some companies may have official policies for how bonuses and such are handled, in the unlikely event that the company stays alive long enough to actually hand them out. If such policies exist, you'll find them in the "employee handbook" or similar document that you will probably be given when you're hired. If you ask around instead, you're likely to receive your fair share of cynical smirks from your co-workers at your naiveté.

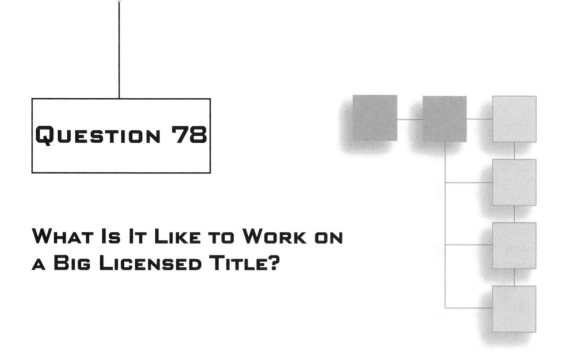

QUESTION 78

WHAT IS IT LIKE TO WORK ON A BIG LICENSED TITLE?

Ian: It's a lot like participating on a 30-person tug-of-war team: You pull as hard as you can and you know you're contributing, but it often feels like you are just one tiny part of a huge effort. This can be good and bad.

For people who love working on these kinds of games, the perks include that you'll have your name on the credits of something that potentially millions of people will play, a game that you might even see a television ad for, and you can say that yes, you worked on that. Also, as part of a large team, you'll be working with loads of talented, awesome people.

The worst part is the feeling that you don't really have much control over the outcome of the game; sure, you can make those textures for the main character's socks look outstanding or whatever, but you are not going to make or break the game, and your contributions will probably not stand out or be noticed by anyone. Also, large projects tend to take a while to complete, usually in the range of two to five years. Working on the same project for so long can cause project burnout; by the time it's done, you will be beyond ready to move on to something new (and if that "something new" is the sequel . . . well, all I can say is, I hope you really like that game franchise).

Additionally, if the IP is licensed from outside the developer and is already well-known, this often contains some excitement if most of the development team are fans, especially if you are given creative license to create a new story within this world. On the other hand, with big-name licenses, the licensors (that is, the people who own the IP) are often protective of their valuable property. There may be a review process where the licensor looks at some aspects of your game and approves them or suggests changes. Some of the changes may seem to make no sense from a game-play perspective, or may necessitate major shifts in direction, which can be pretty frustrating when you feel like seemingly-random outside forces are further chipping away at your contribution to a game.

Brenda: In a sense, every game is a "big name IP," or it has the potential to be. Right from the outset, the creative director or game designer should lay the creative ground rules for the game so that everyone knows what arena they are working in and everything in the game works to strengthen that IP. For instance, a game set in Medieval Ireland wouldn't feature crocodiles as monsters nor would an FPS set in NYC feature people riding on tractors. Licensed IPs are no different, except that their rules come with the IP. In many cases, these rules make little sense. For instance, it's not uncommon for certain stars to agree to be in a series, but prohibit certain behaviors or representations. This extends to the game, naturally. So, licensed IPs featuring known characters often amount to special case code (some can, some can't) or a "lowest common denominator" form of design, which only includes a behavior set that is acceptable to everyone.

Licensed IPs also tend to have specific, highly inflexible release schedules should they coincide with a movie. Your game will ship, regardless of which state it is in. I've also heard about certain studios hiring multiple developers to make a single title, choosing the best one shortly before the date of launch, and canceling the other title at the last minute.

Licensed IPs have royalties built into the project for all kinds of things—authors, music, actors, and so on—and this leaves less money for development. Generally, this only affects smaller developers who accept gigs and are forced to make do with smaller budgets in order to get higher profile projects. Ultimately, I think people working on an IP are hoping to meet the stars and big names behind it. Rarely is that the case, especially for the rank-and-file employees. Making a big name IP is like making any other game, except there's more pressure.

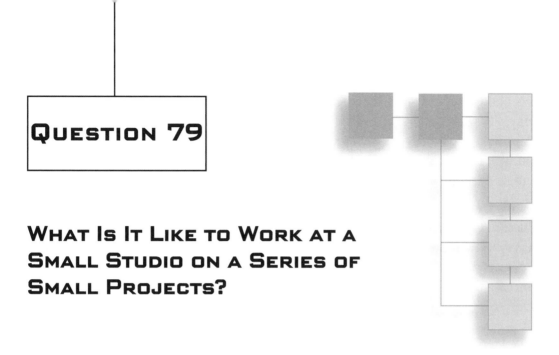

QUESTION 79

WHAT IS IT LIKE TO WORK AT A SMALL STUDIO ON A SERIES OF SMALL PROJECTS?

Ian: As you might guess, it's the opposite of working at a large studio on a single long project (see previous question) in a lot of ways. People are very close, which means that getting along with your co-workers is much more important. Since there are never enough people to go around, expect to "wear a lot of hats" as people say (that is, expect to have a wider variety of job roles and responsibilities than what you are formally trained for). There is rarely any time for rest—by the time you finish one project there is another waiting to go. On the other hand, you also never work on a single game for so long that you get sick of it, and even if you did, you'll at least know that the current project will be over soon.

Brenda: Having worked on both small teams and large teams (and even giant teams), I choose a small team any day. Small teams are faster and more agile, and the development experience is simply far more fun than it otherwise would be when you're all working on a tiny piece of some much greater whole. That said, this is a phenomenally personal preference. There are lots of game developers who prefer working on large teams.

Alex Kain (2007, Designer, Venan Games): For somebody like me, who's always interested in tackling a new idea or concept, the small studio is a fantastic place to work. We often have a couple projects going on at once, split between independent titles we've conceived internally and contract projects that range all over the spectrum. In a little over three years at Venan, I've worked on over 15 titles ranging from basketball sims to space shooters. I'll come in one day and be building a city in *Crazy Taxi*, and the next day, I'll be writing help text for a digital adaptation of *Monopoly*. If I'd been working at a larger studio, I could have easily been working on a single game this entire time.

Aside from the project diversity, it's also nice to have a small studio where you can get to know everybody in the studio, from QA all the way up to the CEO. That's opposed to a 300+ person mega-studio, where you might only get to know people in your same discipline or project team. If I was a designer at Activision, I probably wouldn't get any face time with Bobby Kotick unless I was in trouble. At Venan, everybody talks with everybody, every day—even the CEO. It's just a more positive, open atmosphere, and I really enjoy working in that kind of environment.

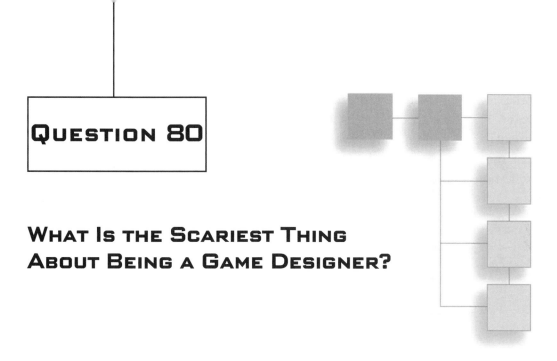

QUESTION 80

WHAT IS THE SCARIEST THING ABOUT BEING A GAME DESIGNER?

Ian: As a game designer, you are ultimately responsible for the player experience. If the game that ships isn't fun, that is your fault and no one else's (well, aside from your fellow designers). Having this kind of responsibility is terrifying enough, before you consider that the actual implementation of the game is left to programmers, artists, musicians, and all kinds of other people who are not working as designers, and these people are relying on you to tell them what to make. So you had better be right.

Hopefully, you can see why many game companies are reluctant to hire game designers with no former experience. It's scary for the people who would hire you, too.

Brenda: Yes. And I am mostly not kidding. Being a game designer means awesomeness—someone is paying thousands or millions of dollars to make your vision come true. Being a game designer is also a terrifying amount of responsibility—someone is RISKING thousands or millions of dollars to make your vision come true. If you screw up, like Ian said, you can blame a hundred different people, but ultimately, history will remember you, and your name will be tied to the failed product forever. That's why it is important, in part, to make sure you join a solid team that not only plays games but has experience shipping successful games, too. Aside from the general responsibility, the scariest moments for me are always when a system comes together but is not fun. It just fails in some way, and in studying the failure, I cannot immediately see what's wrong. In these moments, I always feel the weight of responsibility the most. I go back to the core statement of the game (the one thing the game is about) and try to find out what's getting in the way or why it's having no impact (or too much). I could write a book on designing to a core experience, but Question #80 is not the place to do it.

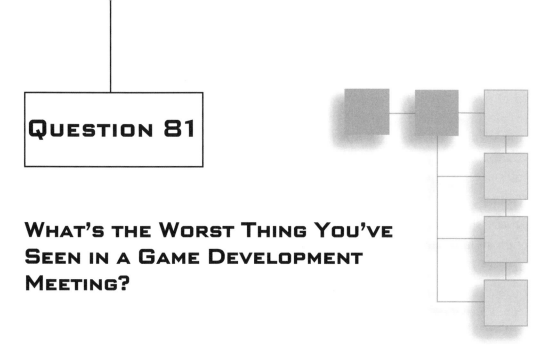

QUESTION 81

WHAT'S THE WORST THING YOU'VE SEEN IN A GAME DEVELOPMENT MEETING?

Ian: I need to provide some background for my worst-day-in-the-office-ever story. The day was September 12, 2001—the day after the planes hit the towers. It didn't help that our office was just down the street from a military air base, so right around the time everyone is expecting planes to fly into buildings, we're hearing air traffic a few hundred feet overhead throughout the day. So everyone was a bit on edge to begin with.

Into this situation, a meeting with the project team was called to address a problem. You see, our game was an online trading-card game set in the future, and one of the cards depicted a plane hitting a building (the text on the card made it clear that a computer hacker was hacking in to a local air traffic control tower and rerouting planes into buildings). We had the means to change the card, but we also had a long-standing official policy of not changing cards from older sets, and this card was on the "never ever change" list. These are the kinds of game design decisions that weigh on a lead designer's shoulders, so if you have fantasies of being that kind of "idea person" some day, just ask yourself if you'd like to be the one responsible for making the final call on something like this.

At any rate, the entire team was invited to brainstorm opinions and ideas. At one point, one team member (a staunch Democrat) made some disparaging comments about President GW Bush and his handling of the situation; another team member (a staunch Republican) was highly offended. The two nearly came to physical blows. I don't know how, exactly, but I somehow managed to keep my head, separate the two of them, and remind them both that they are on the same team and that this wasn't the time or place for divisiveness, and they calmed down. (And yes, you can bet I brought that story up at future job interviews when I was asked how I respond to team conflict!)

And if you think that sounds like a difficult experience, I'm sure there are many others in the industry with horror stories that make my little tale seem tame in comparison. Brenda, for example.

Brenda: Bear in mind that I've been in the industry 30 years, now, so I've probably seen more than the average person would. Still, it's been an amazing ride, and while I've witnessed and heard plenty of horror stories, the reality is that making games is still the single greatest thing you can do. That said, my worst experience in a development meeting is a toss up—I've seen a lead coder throw a chair at another coder. It missed. Another unbelievable moment occurred when a game's production was stopped—a game on which people had invested a lot of their time and creativity—with an offhand, casual remark from the CEO, "Sorry dudes!" The team walked away, unsure of what to do, none of their feelings taken into account. If you don't think that stuff matters and matters a lot, wait until you've had a game cancelled. People get really invested in their projects. I've yet to see a layoff or a product cancellation which did not also involve tears. I've also been a part of far too many "design by committee" meetings, which are painful for all involved, but mostly for the game itself. Design by committee is similar to grenade by the blind.

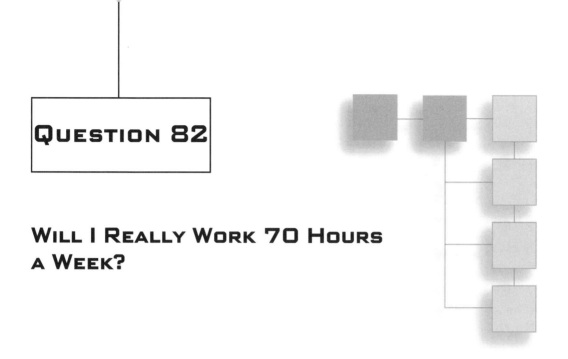

Question 82

Will I Really Work 70 Hours a Week?

Ian: This varies from company to company. Some companies make every effort to minimize overtime, only slipping into "crunch" occasionally if at all, whereas others operate as if they're designed to have people working long hours constantly. It's up to you to figure out what kind of company it is during the interview, before you accept a job there.

Some people I talk to, particularly bright-eyed hopeful students who have not been through this "meat grinder" process yet, wonder why this matters. If you love making games for 40 hours per week, shouldn't you love it twice as much if you get to do the same thing for 80 hours? And anyway, if your goal is to "break in" to the industry, shouldn't you take any job you can get just so you have experience ... and then you can just jump to another job that has a more reasonable schedule?

To answer that first question, at first you might love it ... but over time, working long hours takes its toll. Eventually, you may want to have some kind of life outside work, and if you spend all waking hours there, you'll find it hard to pursue romantic relationships or attempt any kind of family life, or even just find time to play games for pleasure like you used to. Or perhaps you'll just start to feel taken advantage of, as if your company should be paying you a little bit more if they're going to take so many hours of your time. The thrill of working in games wears off quickly under the harsh condition of extended crunch time.

As for the second question, if you are sufficiently desperate to get your first game industry job, taking a job with poor working conditions is certainly one strategy. However, keep in mind that the best time to hunt for a new job is when you still have your old one … but in this case, you'll find it difficult to spend time on a job search when you are spending so much time at your job. As you probably know, job-hunting is exhausting work, and you may just not have the energy for it if your day job is too demanding.

Brenda: Know the law and do your research. California mandates time-and-a-half pay for salaried individuals working in the game industry (and other computer industry) who make less than a particular amount (California Labor Code §515.5). Other states have different regulations. Almost all products require some degree of extra hours (particularly if you have to hit Christmas), so if you are unwilling to do overtime, odds are this is not the industry for you. That said, do your research and know which companies are chronic abusers of overtime and rely on it to ship products. The information is more readily available than you might think. Even following developers' Twitter feeds can reveal patterns in companies. In my career, I have done lots of crunch time. The best comes when you are working with great friends making a great game toward a specific goal and are doing so voluntarily. The worst comes when someone mandates you do a bunch of extra time for no clear goal at all.

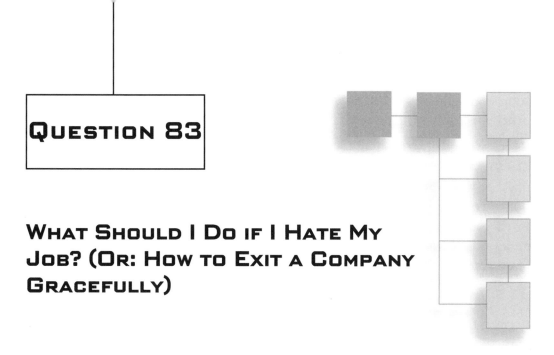

QUESTION 83

WHAT SHOULD I DO IF I HATE MY JOB? (OR: HOW TO EXIT A COMPANY GRACEFULLY)

Ian: As with any job, there will be good times and bad times. The first thing to do is to take a step back and decide whether there is really more bad than good in your current job, or whether you're just in the middle (or near the end) of a rough spot that will clear up soon. After all, you don't want to throw away a perfectly good opportunity just because you're having a bad day. No one but you can know this for sure, but there are a few warning signs:

- If you find yourself acting out towards your co-worker or otherwise engaging in behaviors that seem unlike you

- If the statement "making games is fun!" sounds sarcastic or patronizing to you

- If you are having physical symptoms of stress or are feeling chronically anxious or depressed in a way that requires you to see a doctor or therapist, or you are considering doing the same

If you decide that it really is time to exit, the next step is to decide whether it is the current job or the entire career that is the problem. If it is just your current company that is driving you nuts, and you'd be fine in a better environment, it's time to go job-hunting at better places. On the bright side, in this case, you have a lot of advantages. You've been burned enough that you can probably detect some warning signs of badness during future interviews. You've got industry experience, which will make future job hunts a little easier.

Perhaps most of all, you still have your current job. This may not sound like a blessing, but it offers you two important advantages. First, you still have a paycheck and at least short-term job security, which means during your off hours, you can look for work with relatively little pressure, compared to a time when you're unemployed with rapidly dwindling cash reserves. Second, there's an adage in the industry that it's easiest to find a job if you already have one. Since you haven't quit, been fired, or been laid off, you come across immediately as a strong candidate with no red flags (no one might think that you were let go for good reason). Since you don't technically *need* a new job, you can also make it clear that you're applying for the job because you *want* to work at that particular company and not because you're just desperate to break in with any old job. This puts you in a position of power when it comes to negotiating.

One thing you will want to be *very* careful of is that it is a small industry, and the chances are good that word will get back to your employer if you're not careful. How do you know that the person interviewing you for a new position doesn't just happen to be friends with your current boss? Be discreet; do not put "looking for work" as your Facebook status, for example. And whatever you do, don't perform your job hunt from work; not only do you stand a good chance of getting found out, but it's poor form to be spending company time looking for a job.

Lastly, again since it is a small industry, do your best to exit gracefully. The standard for leaving is four week's notice (or double that if you're a lead). Most any future employer who wants to hire you will be willing to wait at least that long. Consider the timing of your departure; leaving the day before a big milestone, or in the middle of a project when you're on the critical path, is something that will be remembered and that will follow you for the rest of your career. Go out on a high note, making sure you finish all of your assigned tasks or hand them off to others, and be prepared to make yourself available on a limited basis after you leave in case you left a mess behind that you need to clean up. If there is an exit interview, simply say that you stumbled into an opportunity you couldn't turn down; this is not the time to blast anyone or burn bridges.

Brenda: The industry has some general rules of thumb that apply when moving from one gig or another:

- **Never ever trash your current employer or previous employers when interviewing for your new gig.** This throws up all kinds of red flags to prospective employers. Is this how you will talk about them, too? Think about how you will explain your exit before you're sitting in front of an interviewer. Remember, you are interviewing with these people because you're excited to work with them, not because you hate the people you're with (although both may be true).

- **Try not to leave in the middle of a project.** There's a general rule in the game industry that, unless something is going drastically wrong, you do not leave in the middle of a project. If you do, something better be dramatically wrong. However, if a project starts after you declare your intent to leave, and you're assigned to it (or are even assigned to *lead* it), your employers made that move with full knowledge that you'd soon be on your way. Obviously, this doesn't apply to the "live" product space.

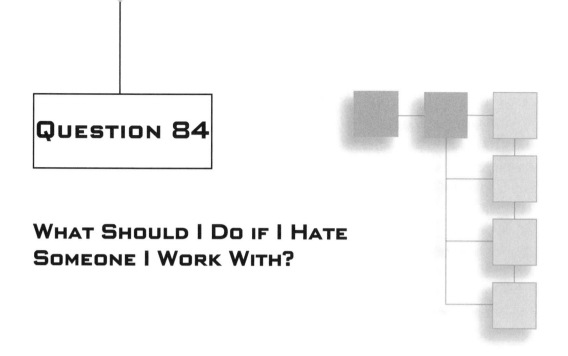

QUESTION 84

WHAT SHOULD I DO IF I HATE SOMEONE I WORK WITH?

Ian: Much as you might like to fantasize, hiring a ninja assassin is not the preferred form of conflict resolution in the game industry.

First, since this can be an explosive situation that harms you as much as anyone, play cautiously. Is there a pattern, or is the other person just having a bad day? If someone treated you harshly once because they were frustrated, but it doesn't happen again (or only happens rarely), it may not be a problem you need to fix. If this is something that happens a lot, explore further.

If a co-worker or boss is chronically doing something that bugs you, the next step should be to honestly assess what role you are playing in the situation. Perhaps they are reacting to you or you are overreacting to them. If you treat someone rudely and then they act rude back, maybe you can change your own behavior and fix the problem without the need to confront anyone. If your lead or boss is treating you negatively, is it because they are mean, or is your work subpar? Think of things you can change about yourself proactively. Also, consider things that you should just accept. Sometimes, one person's laughter can completely grate on you. Are you really going to be able to change that?

If you are convinced that another person needs to change their ongoing behavior, and realize this is a difficult task, first approach them directly if at all possible. Be polite, explain what they're doing, and ask nicely for them to change their behavior as a favor to you. This will solve a surprising number of problems. If you have a reputation for being kind and respectful to those around you, your co-workers will generally return the favor.

If that fails, or if you're talking about a personality conflict where the other person just rubs you the wrong way and it's not any specific behavior, the next step is to go to your boss or lead and mention the problem. It helps here to not try to place blame, and to shoulder some of the responsibility yourself; you are the one who is doing the hating, after all. It helps to mentally frame the issue as one that *you* have, because you may very well be the one with the issue. For instance, I have asked other coders for help in mentoring a junior coder to work better with designers—how can I do a better job?

Other times, the issue is a clearly problematic one. Suggest solutions, such as being put on a different team or working with different people, to minimize your exposure. For example, Brenda once worked in a situation where a co-worker was frequently explosive. She eventually left the company for different reasons, but management did not address the issue. While she was there, she steered clear of the projects he was on, and asked that he not be appointed to a lead role on her team. If even this is not possible, you'll have to decide how important the job is to you. As a last resort, consider seeking work elsewhere (see Question #83).

Incidentally, the best defense against being forced to work with someone you can't stand is to pay attention during the job interview. Do you get to meet everyone on the team, or at least everyone who you'll be working closely with? Do they seem friendly? Do you notice anything that just seems "off" or feels wrong about them, even if you can't put your finger on it? Is someone actively rude to you during your interview? Do you get asked a lot of questions in the interview about how you handle interpersonal conflict, suggesting that conflicts may happen often? Remember during your interview that this is your chance to meet the people with whom you will be spending a lot of time. You'll probably spend more time with your project team than anyone else, even your spouse or family, so take the time to make sure you'll get along before you make a commitment!

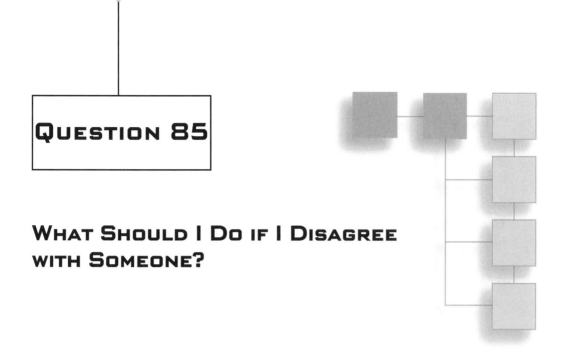

QUESTION 85

WHAT SHOULD I DO IF I DISAGREE WITH SOMEONE?

Ian: The game industry is full of creative people who are passionate about their work and can be very opinionated about how to make the game they're working on into the best possible release product. It's inevitable that there will be differences of opinion, and how you handle these disagreements can be the difference between a development grind and a development joy.

First, it's time to eat some humble pie. There are a few general truths that are good to repeat to yourself, whenever you start feeling like you have all the answers and the people around you are just being idiots:

- **The people who you work with are *probably* not idiots (or maybe they are—see Brenda's answer next).** Most likely, they are intelligent, passionate, talented people, just like you. If you *are* surrounded by clueless, talentless hacks, ask yourself what you're doing there. If they disagree with you, give them the benefit of the doubt that it is probably for an intelligent reason ... especially if you have already explained your position, and they still disagree.

- **Don't just think of your idea in a vacuum, but within the realistic constraints that the team is operating.** Often, other people disagree with you not because your logic is flawed, but rather because they have additional information that changes the outcome. Maybe that new feature you want to add *would* make the game better, but it would take too long

245

to implement and doesn't fit in the schedule. Maybe the change you want to make to weapon strength *would* make the game more balanced, except that you didn't consider a new subsystem that's getting added later that will change the balance around in unexpected ways. Maybe the new story arc you wrote *would* sound better, except it doesn't fit in with some of the backstory documents that you haven't read yet.

- **Game development is a fast-paced environment.** Sometimes other people may simply tell you "no" without explanation because they don't have time to explain it to you. A full explanation might involve a lot of details and take a lot of time, and they've got a pile of tasks to complete, and they simply can't stop their day just to educate you. You may have to take a few things on faith.

- **If other people on the team are more experienced than you, it may be that you are simply wrong, for reasons that will become clear to you when you gain a little more experience.** It is okay for you to be wrong, of course; your lead may point out the reasons to you, and if not, the game itself certainly will. Most often, you will eventually understand why others did what they did, or that their way of doing it was one of a dozen possible (equally valid ways) to make it work. Bear in mind, it is okay for them to be wrong. It's the responsibility of the lead to point this out, and in the event she fails to, the game most certainly will. Most often, however, you will eventually understand why they did what they did, or that their way of doing it was one of a hundred possible ways, all of which would have worked just as well.

- **If nothing else, keep in mind that whatever it is that you want to argue about, it is probably not as important as you think.** If this is your first game project, try this exercise: During the project, make a list of the ten *most important things* that didn't make it into the game (whether they be features that were never added, changes that weren't made, or bugs that weren't fixed). Then, a year later, look back at your list and see how many of these were noticed by the players or reviewers. Odds are, the answer is almost none of them. When a person works on a project, after a while they have a tendency to not be able to see the "big picture" of the project; this is natural and happens to all of us.

Generally, this is a matter of trust. Do you trust the project leads to know what they're doing, and to make the right call for the overall game? You should, since you are relying on the rest of your team to do their part to build the game. Let your ideas be known, tactfully and conscientiously, but trust the people you are working with to be competent at their jobs even if they disagree with you.

You might wonder, is there ever a time where you *know* something is so important that you *must* bring others around to your way of thinking, even if it means going to war with your team or with a critical member of that team? Brenda has a few real-life examples that illustrate the gravity of the situation that would require such an action. According to Brenda, "Tread super carefully here. In my 30-year career, there have only been three times where I felt such a maneuver was justified." These situations are as follows:

- **The development director was coming in, doing a bit of work, and then repeatedly bailing for an afternoon of golf.** Needless to say, someone needed to know about this. Work was not getting done. He was axed, but still remains in the game industry, astonishingly.

- **The lead programmer was in way over his head and had declared a "no talk" policy with the game designers.** The programmer had only worked on one project before in a lead capacity, and that project was a small web game. Being lead on a game for two consoles was too much pressure. The coder eventually succumbed to that pressure and was replaced, but only after it had done a lot of damage to the team and product.

- **A game designer had too much on his shoulders and was in desperate need of help, but didn't see it.** In this case, the designer was working on a pitch which would be the make or break pitch for a small independent developer. If the external publisher liked it? Everyone kept their jobs. If they didn't? The company would be shut down. The designer carried on, not asking for help, and the powers that be implicitly trusted his vision. Other designers more senior to him could have helped, but he resisted those efforts. In the end, the company was shut down. Whether the vision of others could have helped is unknown, but "cowboying it" is rarely a good path, unless your track record proves you are, well, a cowboy.

At what point does your responsibility to the game and the company outweigh your responsibility to your lead, or your responsibility to keep your nose out of other people's business? If you honestly believe that the project or the entire company itself is in jeopardy if something isn't done about a certain problem, if you are so certain that you are willing to put not just your current job but your entire career at risk, there are a few things you can do.

Talk to your lead and make your case; if he disagrees, you can go above his head to his lead or boss, and so on up to the president of the company . . . but realize that whenever you go over someone's head, you are making a mortal enemy, so you had better be really sure of yourself. You are essentially saying that you know how to do your lead's job better than your lead does. Such a move is putting your entire career at risk, so if you go to this extreme, make sure it is worth it!

Brenda: Ian has already covered most of the bases here, but there are two issues that require more detail. What if you really are working with people who just don't get it at all? This can happen in all kinds of scenarios. Let's say you are a much more experienced developer who has taken a job with a junior team or you're a junior developer who has taken a job with people not familiar with games, but who desire a product that is game-like. In this case, there are only two possible scenarios: educate or bail. Education should be your first path. Explain why you feel the way you do, and take the time to help them understand your needs. I have done many workshops with non-game developers or very junior game developers who found themselves suddenly in a "game company," which was formerly a company making some other kind of software. I have had to explain very basic concepts—the "core," or the concept of game mechanics, for instance—and educate on the reasons why a particular feature would be excellent for or a fatal blow to the core of the game. I've used books, GDC recorded presentations (GDCVault.com), and game design exercises from the book *Challenges for Game Designers* to get the practice and point across. Sometimes, though, bailing may be your only option. If so, you wouldn't be the first person to accept a job and want out. See Question #83.

Another important constraint you should always employ in such situations is this: "Bitch up, not down." Never undermine team morale by complaining to your peers or to the people below you. Nothing can destroy morale or make a solvable problem into an unsolvable one quite like this. Keep your concerns focused and tight and remember to ask yourself, "Does this need to be changed? Does it need to be changed *now*? Does it need to be changed *by me*?" If you find yourself waffling on these points, then do nothing.

I feel it's useful to relate another story here. During development of *Wizardry 8*, a game that went on to win many awards, there were multiple disagreements in the lead's team. Because we'd been making games together for many years, though, we knew when to let something go one way or another, even if we didn't completely agree, largely based on our trust for one another. All these years later, there is only one thing I wish had gone differently. The other points? I've forgotten them all. They just weren't important. So, things seem more important than they really are, and actual play will always reveal the answer sooner than a seven-hour meeting. The key in all this is to have perspective, respect your team, and trust that your lead will do the right thing. It also helps to know that leads have the freedom to fail. If they do, it's on their shoulders.

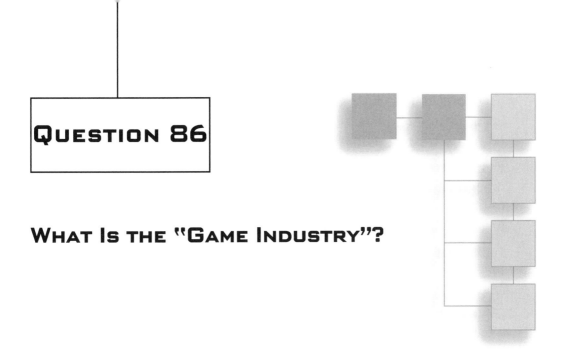

QUESTION 86

WHAT IS THE "GAME INDUSTRY"?

Brenda: It encompasses a lot more than you probably think. When people think of the game industry, they often think of the traditional, hardcore space dominated by AAA titles, giant MMOs, and FPSs. However, the actual game industry is a whole lot bigger than that, and for people looking to break in, that's an important thing to know. There are really six key divisions in which the game industry functions:

- **AAA (pronounced "Triple-A") or traditional:** These games are usually made for consoles or PC, take anywhere from 2–5 years to develop, have teams of 50+ individuals, and have significant budgets.

- **Social and casual:** These games have much smaller teams in the range of 5 to 25, take 4 to 8 months to develop, and have much smaller budgets than their AAA counterparts. Companies in this space have aggressively grown in recent years.

- **Mobile:** This market includes standard mobile phones, smartphones, and tablets. Like social and casual games, these games have smaller budgets, timelines, and teams. Similarly, the market is exploding and poised for growth.

- **Serious:** These games are often developed in response to specific corporate or institutional needs. For example, the game *ReMission* was developed to help children understand what chemotherapy did and why it was important. Many titles are developed each year by the military and others for training purposes.

- **Researchers (or academic developers):** Although not traditionally thought of as a part of the game "industry," an increasing number of institutions support active game developers who work on projects in the university or research context.

- **Indie:** The heart of the game industry; there are more opportunities for indie developers than ever before on mobile platforms, Facebook, major consoles' downloadable sections (like XBLA), and the burgeoning art game community. The solo developers who created *Minecraft* made over a half million dollars in a few short months after release. It is possible for a couple people in a garage to make it big (provided they work their butts off).

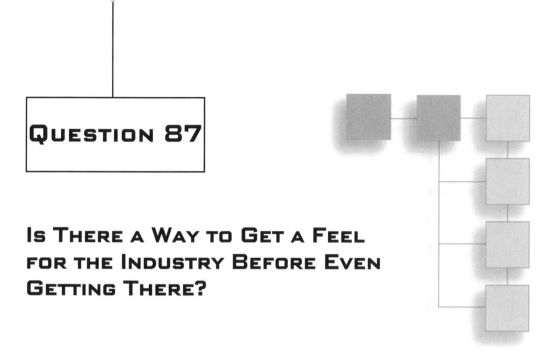

QUESTION 87

IS THERE A WAY TO GET A FEEL FOR THE INDUSTRY BEFORE EVEN GETTING THERE?

Ian: Although nothing is a perfect substitute for the actual job, the best way to immerse yourself in the culture is to attend major industry conferences like GDC. If a sufficient number of game developers are congregating at a particular location and you are there interacting with them, you'll get a pretty good idea of the industry culture.

As for the actual development work, the easiest way to get a feel for that is to participate in some kind of game-making event, such as a contest or game jam. By going through the process, especially if you are working with others on a team, you will experience the highs and lows of a full development cycle.

Brenda: I don't know. This is a tough question, and I think Ian's answer is a good one. At the same time, there is something core about being on a team, working together to ship a game, having gone through that full experience in the industry that gives you an idea of the shared creative experience of which we are all a part. It is that experience and repetition of the same that binds us together in much the same way that (pardon the odd metaphor) addicts and alcoholics in recovery are bound together. We have a shared experience and respect for one another. There are also very different cultures within the industry itself. For instance, the companies in the web app space that are presently making games have cultures that are nothing at all like a traditional game company's culture. Likewise, the culture inside a hardcore FPS studio is different than the studios making MMOs. So much of the culture is present on Twitter. I recommend following a lot of game developers, and you'll see what we're like.

QUESTION 88

IS THE GAME INDUSTRY A GOOD PLACE TO MEET SOMEONE TO DATE?

Ian: The game industry is about 90% white, male, and straight. If that's the kind of person you want to date, you're in luck. If not . . . well, then if you manage to find romance, statistically speaking it will probably be from outside the industry.

All of this is assuming you find any time for a life outside of your job.

Brenda: If your life is all about games, having a partner who is also all about games is pure win. There are actually a lot of women now in the game industry, particularly in the social space. Unless you're in a major game dev hub like San Francisco, Montreal, Austin, or Seattle (and these are just a few of the many hubs worldwide), socializing with other game developers isn't such a common thing. If you're entering games looking for a hook up, there are other professions for you.

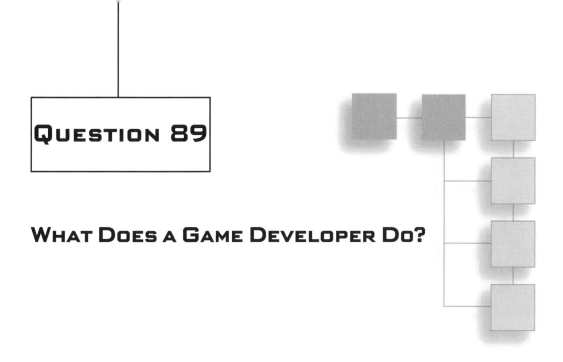

Question 89

What Does a Game Developer Do?

Ian: "Game developer" is a general term used to describe everyone involved with the creation of a game. Saying you are a game developer is like saying that you build skyscrapers for a living; buildings aren't built by individuals, but by teams of specialists. Just as construction projects have their structural engineers, architects, construction workers, and general contractors, game projects have their own specialties:

- **Game designers are to games what architects are to construction.** Designers create the blueprints for the game (called "design documents") that tell the rest of the team what to build. Designers do not necessarily build the game themselves, but they need to be able to articulate the game to others on the team. Other tasks that often fall to game designers are the design of game content (lists of enemies, characters, special moves, items, levels, and so on) and story writing.

- **Programmers are the game equivalent of builders; they take the design documents and turn them into working code.** Without coders, digital games do not happen.

- **Artists are the game equivalent of interior designers and landscapers; they make the game look nice.** Artists create all of the graphics, visuals, and animations in the game.

- **The field of game audio (practitioners might be called sound designers or composers or just game audio people) deals with the sound effects and music in the game.**

- **Producers are the game equivalent of general contractors; their role on a team is to keep the project on budget and on schedule.** Producers may not necessarily do any of the actual development work, but especially on larger teams, they are critical for keeping the team organized and making sure that critical tasks don't fall through the cracks.

- **Lastly, QA (quality assurance) plays the game to discover bugs.** Every non-trivial computer program has some errors somewhere, and it is up to QA to locate and identify these problems so they can be fixed by the rest of the team.

Brenda: In the social game space, or in companies that have transitioned from other web app companies, when one refers to "developers," he or she is generally referring to programmers. Resist it. It takes more than code to develop a game, and in the actual game industry, game developers are as Ian described.

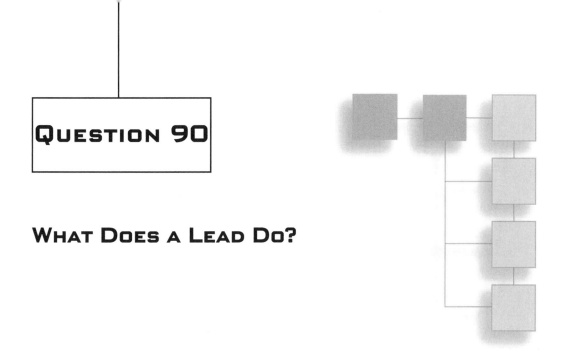

QUESTION 90

WHAT DOES A LEAD DO?

Brenda: Leads are expected to be experts in their discipline, which, since this is the ever-changing game industry, means that they still have a lot to learn. Being lead doesn't mean you are necessarily the best programmer/designer/artist in the company. It means that you are the best suited for the role of lead—an individual with the right blend of design/programming/art skills and people skills to get the job done. I have been a lead since 1994, and in the course of that time, I've done a variety of things.

- **Vision:** The lead designer sets the overall vision for the game and the player experience within it. In some cases such as with larger games, he or she may be lead over a particular system. Other times, the lead may be working at the direction of a creative director who holds that vision. The lead artist works with the game designer to set the artistic vision for the game and determines assignments for each of his or her artists. The lead coder determines the tech necessary to complete the project, creates the code architecture for the game, and assigns each of his coders to develop the various systems.

- **Task assignment:** Your lead knows the things that your group needs to do to finish the game or to finish this particular milestone of the game. He or she will determine the tasks and decide which of his or her reports gets to do them. In my case, I made these assignments based on the person's skill in that particular area or their request to work on them. It's important to give people a chance to grow and learn new things, too.

- **Firewall:** Leads protect the team from incoming garbage from the exec or lead level. You need to keep your people focused and happy on the game and not distracted from the other things that rain down from above.

- **Compliment/critique:** Leads help people grow by never missing an opportunity for a genuine compliment as well as offering genuine critique when it's appropriate. When you are in a role as a lead, you are there because someone viewed your skill set as appropriate for that role. Others can learn from you or will at least rely on you to make sure they can do their best job. Leads are also asked to review and approve the work of others, so they have plenty of opportunity for both compliments and critiques.

- **Manage:** Leads directly manage one or more individuals. That often means approving days off, dealing with periodic personal problems, and knowing when to bring those problems to the attention of people above you. It sometimes also means going to bat for these very same people.

- **Crisis intervention:** Leads need to spot problems before they happen and work to correct them.

- **Crisis management:** Sometimes, leads fail in crisis intervention. When that happens, they need to clean up the mess and resolve the situation.

- **Flotsam:** Leads do so many different things, from meetings to e-mail, to phone calls with the publisher.

These activities generally occupy 40% of the lead's time, leaving the other 60% of the time in which to accomplish their tasks. As a note, if you are the only artist, designer, or coder on a project, do not list yourself as the project's "lead" designer, coder, or artist on your résumé. List yourself as the "sole" whatever. Being a lead implies that you managed others.

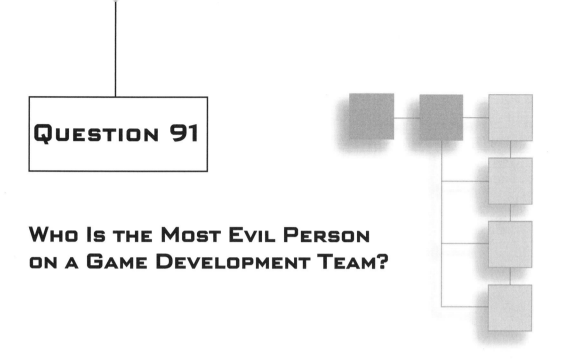

QUESTION 91

WHO IS THE MOST EVIL PERSON ON A GAME DEVELOPMENT TEAM?

Ian: Depends on whom you ask. To a programmer, all game designers are evil because they can't make up their minds about anything, and every time they change their minds it means the programmers have to redo their work. To a game designer, programmers alternate between being evil (when they insist that it's impossible to code your brilliant new mechanic) and godly (when they then proceed to code it anyway in half an hour). Artists and programmers have that natural right brain/left brain personality clash going for them, so at any given time an artist might be convinced that the programmers are crazy, whereas the programmers would state under oath that the artists are insane. Programmers and QA also have this love/hate relationship because a QA person is mostly hired to tell the programmers what they did wrong. Oh, and everyone hates the producer, because they are constantly telling people that there's not enough time or money and that beloved features need to be cut. About the only person on the development team who *isn't* seen as evil is the game audio person, who is instead mostly invisible.

Brenda: So, what Ian says is true. However, there is one person who is more hated than all—the person in power who wants to make changes to the game that make no godly sense at all. Very often, this person is the CEO, the studio head, the external VP of HooHa, or a PM (the social industry's term for a producer who also fills the role of a game designer). Unfortunately, what the person says goes, and no matter what you think, you will encounter such a person, and they will affect your game, like it or not. Unless you have a strong lead with a will of steel, that person in power will be hated. When this happens to you, spend about 10 minutes dwelling on it, and then make a good game anyway. There are many people in the game industry, a lot of awesome things to do, and there's no point in wasting time or talent on such things. Also, if you find yourself in an unwinnable, unbreakable scenario like this, it might be time to look for another gig. Life's also too short to get paid to argue.

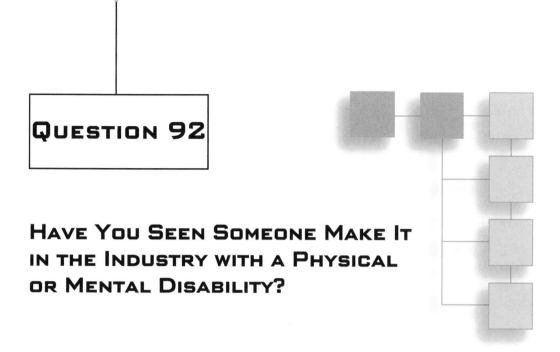

QUESTION 92

HAVE YOU SEEN SOMEONE MAKE IT IN THE INDUSTRY WITH A PHYSICAL OR MENTAL DISABILITY?

Brenda: You name it, and at least one prominent person in the game industry has it. In some cases these appear to even be a net positive. Multiple prominent people in the industry have Asperger's syndrome. OCD is certainly not uncommon. Depression, addiction, alcoholism, everything. I know many people who have been affected by them. Likewise, developers with a whole range of disabilities are in the industry and are making an impact just like the rest of us. We do, however, have a ways to go. If this is of interest to you as a developer and a player of games, check out the IGDA's Accessibility SIG, which actively works to make the industry and games better for those with disabilities.

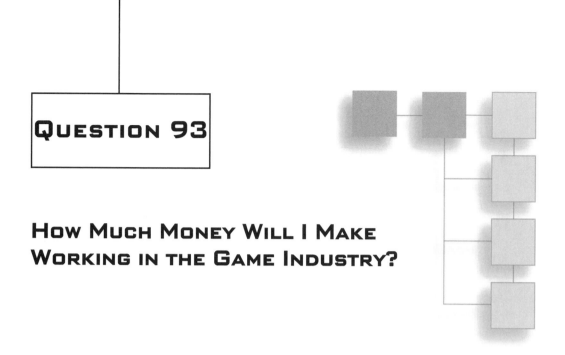

QUESTION 93

HOW MUCH MONEY WILL I MAKE WORKING IN THE GAME INDUSTRY?

Ian: If making money is your primary concern, do not work in the game industry. A programmer working for an enterprise software development studio will generally make more money than an otherwise equivalent game programmer. An artist can make more in movies, television, or advertising. A game designer or producer can rename their job title to "systems analyst" or "project manager" and double their salary in the software industry. A game audio person can make more by playing their guitar for loose change on the subway. Do the job because you love it, not because you think it'll make you rich. (Sure, occasionally you do hear of individuals who make obscene amounts of money making games. Those are newsworthy specifically because they are so rare.) Your worth will also scale dramatically based on the caliber of your work and your specialization. Graphics and engine coders can make a significant chunk of change. Designers with previous successful titles also can do well.

Okay, you say, but can you at least make a living wage doing game development? Absolutely. If you want a numerical salary range, here's what you do:

1. Use the search engine of your choice to find the latest copy of the Annual Salary Survey, administered by *Game Developer Magazine*. This is a survey sent out to game developers each year, asking them questions like how long they've been in the industry, what is their job title, and how much they make.

2. Laugh at the survey, because the numbers are grossly inflated. Partly this is because the industry is highly concentrated in California, where salaries have to be high because you have to pay $2,000/month to rent a broom closet. Partly this is because game developers inflate their salaries when responding to the survey because they want to show it to their boss in the hopes that they'll get a raise, even though they know this won't work.

3. Reduce the numbers by a percentage that sounds reasonable to you, and then adjust for the cost of living in your area. Use an online cost of living calculator to get a feel for how different the numbers are in various geographical regions. Actually, use several calculators, because they'll all give slightly different numbers, and take an average.

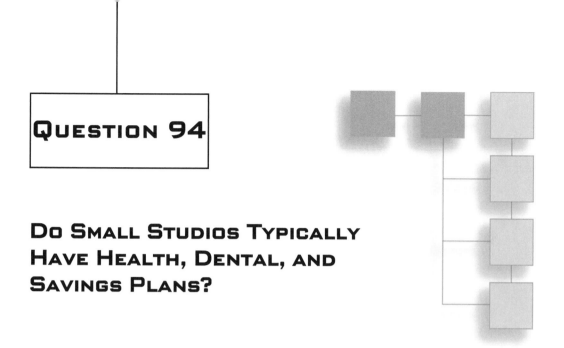

QUESTION 94

DO SMALL STUDIOS TYPICALLY HAVE HEALTH, DENTAL, AND SAVINGS PLANS?

Ian: Small studios typically either go out of business or get acquired by large studios, so the last thing you should be worried about is benefits (your greater concern might be whether you'll have a job next month). That said, for the companies I've worked for in the U.S., health, dental, and 401(k) are pretty common (and as of the printing of this book, the *Game Developer Magazine's* annual salary survey shows that across disciplines, virtually all full-time developers get these benefits). The exception would be part-time work (such as QA) or contract/freelance work, which tends not to come with any benefits other than pay.

Brenda: Yes, they have everything the larger studios have, and sometimes more because they are so eager to get employees. In Silicon Valley, you will find companies who will even get your clothing laundered and give you hair cuts at work. To new game devs, this seems like a dream come true. To veterans, this is merely another way of saying, "We never want you to leave the office."

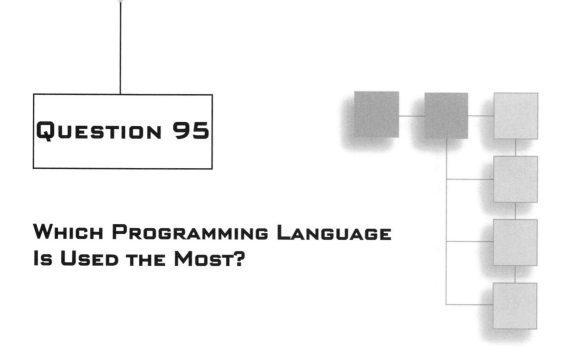

QUESTION 95

WHICH PROGRAMMING LANGUAGE IS USED THE MOST?

Ian: It depends. For the majority of AAA (big-budget) game development—that is, the big retail release titles you see on PC and console—you can expect to see C++ as the main weapon of choice. Social media games are created in Flash. Mobile games vary by platform, but are usually some kind of C++ or Java derivative.

Many games use some kind of scripting language, such as Python or Lua, for those parts of the gameplay that are changed by the designers a lot. As long as you're learning to program, picking up a scripting language or two along the way is not a horrible thing.

Here's the good news: Just about all of these languages are derived from C/C++ in some fashion, so if you learn any one of them, it is much easier to pick up and learn another. By the time you learn three or four languages, you will see so many similarities that picking up a new one will be second nature . . . which is a good thing, considering how often the technology changes.

Brenda: In the social space, the dominant language is Flash. Oddly enough, I've seen many senior coders who could easily handle 6502 Assembly turned away because they didn't yet know Flash. This, I think, is to the determent of the social game industry, since for many game industry coders, adding Flash to their lexicon of languages simply isn't that challenging.

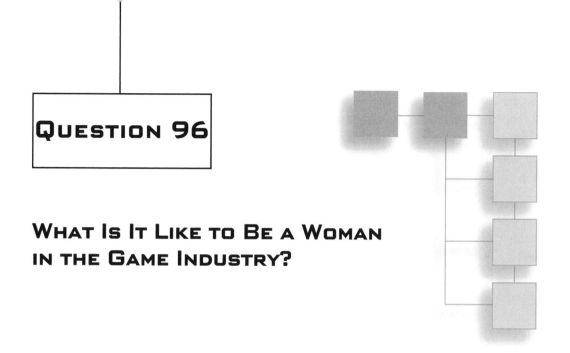

QUESTION 96

WHAT IS IT LIKE TO BE A WOMAN IN THE GAME INDUSTRY?

Brenda: I get asked this question a lot, actually, and you know what? It's been great. In my 30 years in the industry, it has been nothing but a positive thing for me. In fact, the number of interviews I have done solely because I am a woman must be over 100 at this point. That said, there certainly are not an overwhelming number of women in this industry. When I first started, I could count the number of female game designers on a single hand. Nowadays, there are many, many of us, and at GDC, the rooms that host the IGDA's Women In Games Special SIG are often overflowing! Although we may still be small, we are a well-networked and tight group of individuals. Join the IGDA's Women's SIG mailing list, introduce yourself, and jump in. It's a great place to start. I also encourage you to work with a fellow female mentor or reach out to a known game developer to ask her questions as you head off on your career. I've had women ask me everything from how to deal with a co-worker's x-rated photos to what to do if they have no place for you to nurse at the office. I'm always glad to help and to share experience as are many other women in this industry. In recent years, particularly with the rise in social gaming, it's never been a better time to be a woman. Companies are realizing the need for a diverse workforce more than ever, and female game designers, coders, and artists are actively sought after. After all, the average player of a social game is a woman in her 40s!

Is it all a rosy picture? No. There have been notorious cases where female developers were singled out and sexualized by idiots, which caused a lot of embarrassment and pain for the developer in question. Furthermore, virtually every time an article runs on female developers, the comments section turns into a ranking fest that I often refuse to even read. Mind you, this is more a function of the audience for some types of games than the industry itself. I've also heard stories ranging from strippers in the office (or meetings held at strip clubs) to pictures of naked women by male developers' desks. These situations end up being phenomenally awkward things to resolve for developers (both male and female) who don't want such things in the workplace. Inevitably, bringing it up with the person in question or with HR always ends well and not well—the image goes down or the strippers don't reappear, but no one feels particularly good about how that came to be. I think that's why it pays to find out all you can about a company's culture before you go in. Ask around before you even apply.

Question 97

What Is It Like to Be a Minority in the Game Industry? Is Diversity Important?

Manveer Heir (2005, Senior Designer, BioWare): This industry is homogeneous, especially the North American dev scene. It is largely skewed to being white, male. The concept of knowing how to use computers skews the economics to being middle to upper class. We have a large number of the same types of people from the same types of backgrounds in our industry. That doesn't mean all of them are the same. That doesn't mean they don't deserve to be in the industry. That doesn't mean they should  apologize or feel guilty. It's not a "white man's" problem that he is doing what he loves. All I am stating is that the industry is homogeneous.

My next statement is that this is, ultimately, a problem. Anyone who saw me and others talk about race in game characters at DICE and GDC last year can tell you that statistically we under-represent minorities as a whole in games, and that includes women. My hypothesis as to why this exists is that we come from similar backgrounds. We all have biases, but if a group of developers has similar upbringings and experiences, it's very possible and likely they have similar ideas. Think about how often you are working on a game and someone mentions an idea that basically is from *Star Wars* or *Alien* or some other popular geek culture—we rip off the same movies and books all the time. That happens because we all share those experiences in this industry and they are common and so therefore we are influenced by them. But what if we had more people who were influenced by other things? Who grew up another way? Who have a feminine point of view? Who grew up with a different culture or religion? I think it's perfectly reasonable to want a more diverse workforce and therefore more diverse types of games—and I don't mean games for women or minorities. Rather, I mean games that aren't about white space marines saving the world for the umpteenth time. How many times do I have to play and do the same thing? This isn't about fairness … it's about having more interesting and different game experiences instead of having the same experience over and over.

So this is fixed by diversifying the workforce. Except, for many minorities and women, they don't even know this is an option. Many white men know you can make video games for a living. Many minorities don't. Having visible figures to look up to in an industry increases exposure. But usually you look up to people who are like you in some way and, this has been shown in academic studies, that includes gender and color of skin. In other words, women and minorities are less likely to be inspired by a white man who succeeds at something than they are by someone who is like them succeeding. So awards or recognitions for being a woman, or Hispanic, or Indian, or Black, or whatever are important. We're talking about increasing exposure so that maybe one day, when I retire, some kid entering the field of games can talk about different women and minorities who inspired them. And then hopefully, over time, the demographics will shift and we'll start having more unique, expressive, and different types of games.

I don't expect most developers to agree with me. The topics of race and gender are polarizing, and we're trained to react strongly to them. Most people made their minds up about this a long time ago. If you aren't going to reconsider your position, I implore you to show some understanding. Most of all, I implore you to understand that that there are many of us in the industry who feel out of place and who feel like we can't express ourselves (without starting our own companies) fully because our viewpoint isn't shared, since our viewpoint is colored by our upbringing. Allow us to grow, allow us to diversify, allow us to celebrate those that excel who aren't exactly the same so that they can inspire the next generation of developers into becoming game developers.

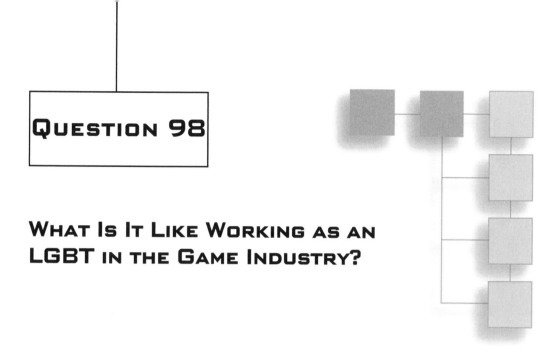

QUESTION 98

WHAT IS IT LIKE WORKING AS AN LGBT IN THE GAME INDUSTRY?

Ian: Not nearly as hostile as, say, serving in the military. True story: I have worked with more game designers who are LGBT than those who aren't, so I don't even think of this as a minority in any sense. As often as not, I'm the token straight guy on the design team. I'm sure my experience is an anomaly, but it never bothered me or anyone else on the team, as far as I've seen. If I've seen any open hostility towards LGBT developers, it has come from the player community in online games, not from the developer community. That said ... well, the fact that two of the three contributors for this question requested anonymity, that probably says something as well.

Ben Rex Furneaux (2007, Designer, Turbulenz): As a child of the 80s, I grew up playing games like *Duke Nukem* much of the time. Just as I became very good at hiding my sexuality, I became equally adept at hiding the type of games I was playing from my parents. Whilst I took great pleasure from saving the world, I can distinctly remember not loving the pixilated breasts being thrust onto my beige monitor (which in some ways helped affirm the fact I was gay, or at least that I had a severe dislike for lack of clarity in erotic images).

In my early 20s, I'd always been incredibly comfortable with my sexuality around friends, family, and peers, yet when I began to look for a games art job in 2007, I became wary of entering what I expected to be an industry dominated by straight males. I was concerned the male/female gender balance would make it difficult to fit in or relate to team members. I certainly never expected to meet another LGBT game developer.

My expectations were wrong—and to this date, everyone I have worked with has respected and embraced my sexuality. I've been honored to work with and meet many exceptional gay and lesbian role models within the games industry.

In the last four years, I have felt I can be open about my sexuality and that I am embraced by colleagues for my openness and diversity. I'm happy I work in a liberal, diverse culture filled with people who are equally as weird, quirky, and creative as I am.

"Tiffany" (2002, Producer): I am happy to report that I have never experienced (at least that I know of) any discrimination or negativity in the workplace based on sexual orientation. I've had the great fortune of living in the Bay Area for many years, so that could be a reason, or perhaps it's just that attitudes have shifted over the past couple of decades in general. The industry also has a constant influx of younger people and a great many creative people, so this is likely a factor as well. I should also mention that I spent time living and working in Austin, Texas, and had a very good experience there, too.

What I've found about the games industry is that people tend to be much more concerned about your work product and how good of an employee you are rather than what you do in your personal life. When you do a great job, people respect that and respond to it.

At each workplace, my partner has been invited and happily welcomed at company functions. I have never been the only "out" person at a game company—there have always been at least a couple of other openly gay people. I have encountered more lesbians on the whole than gay men, and a number of people who identify as bisexual.

I've been happy to see more out gay people getting involved with the industry over the years, and I really hope this will continue. It's a positive thing all around when we can remind our colleagues that gay people do indeed love games and are a part of the buying audience. Historically, there has been a tendency to overlook, forget, or simply ignore this. It's good when we can be in a position to challenge assumptions and influence content decisions, even if it's just to question and discuss ideas that are potentially offensive or not inclusive.

Anonymous (2008, Programmer): Some background: I discovered games in 1981 as a teenager, and I immediately became enthralled with games such as *Wizardry* (not a plug for Brenda, it really was a big obsession of mine for quite a while—enough so that my friends teased me about it). Being more-or-less geeky and into such things as *Dungeons and Dragons*, I built character and dungeon and map generators, and eventually combined them into a game. In the early 90s, a friend and I had an idea to make it multiplayer over the quickly-growing Internet. We wrote up a detailed business plan and technical plan, and brought it to a venture capital firm in San Diego, who eventually denied funding.

I still wanted to get into the game industry, but it always seemed that the jobs paid about half of what I could get doing enterprise development or consulting. As I got older (around 30), I still longed to be in the game industry and went to the Art Institute in San Francisco to study game art and design, where I excelled while maintaining a full-time job writing shipping software (not exactly exciting). I applied for several game development jobs, trying to impress that my 10+ years of development experience combined with my art school experience would make me a great game developer, but no one bit. I felt as though I was being judged for being a woman in a world where women aren't coders ... especially not game developers.

During interviews, I was often "reminded" that I would be working with a bunch of boys, and then asked if was I okay with that. Of course I was okay with that! That's the nature of the game industry! I never got any of those jobs, even though I had years of experience making solid applications and leading teams.

Over the next several years, my gender identity shifted, and I started exhibiting a more "butch" appearance. I tried again to apply for a game development job, and voilà! I was a shoe-in. I really believe that outwardly showing my "butchness" was what got me in. It's at least what made people get over the idea that a woman couldn't be a good coder. Being a queer woman was always less of an issue than being a woman.

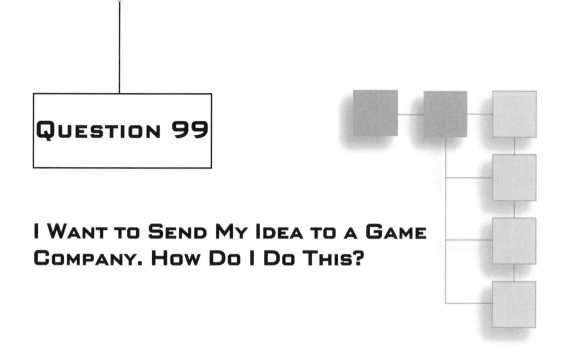

QUESTION 99

I WANT TO SEND MY IDEA TO A GAME COMPANY. HOW DO I DO THIS?

Ian: You don't.

But you want to. How can you *possibly* get your *amazing idea* made if you don't submit it to a company? And why would they turn down your idea when it will *obviously* make them *so much money*?

For one thing, there's the legal system. If they so much as *look* at your idea and then they happen to come out with a game that has even a superficial resemblance, you might sue them. Game companies know this, so many of them will flat out refuse to look at anything you've done. If they *do* look at your work, it will probably only be after they have you sign a release form that signs away all of your rights to the idea, which probably defeats the purpose of sending it in.

Also, "ideas" are worthless in the industry. Just like everyone in Hollywood has a "brilliant" movie script they're working on (including the janitors), everyone in the game industry has at least one "brilliant" idea for a game. Ideas are the easy part; actually building the game is the long, hard, and expensive part. Give the same "brilliant idea" to ten different teams, and you'll get ten very different products. Ideas are nothing; execution is everything. A wonderful idea, horribly implemented, loses money.

If you want your game made, go forth and make it. If you don't have the expertise, you can learn the skills you are missing, or try to team up with

279

someone else who can provide those skills (but you will have to convince them that it is worth their time to work on *your* idea, rather than their own idea, and the burden of proof is on you since you're asking for their time). If you have a working game, and the game is fun, *that* will get people's attention much more than an idea.

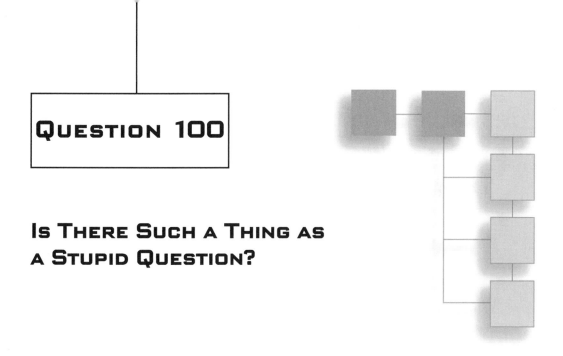

QUESTION 100

IS THERE SUCH A THING AS A STUPID QUESTION?

Ian: The adage that "there is no such thing as a stupid question" or "the only stupid question is the one that's not asked" is true for the classroom, but not so much when talking with a game developer whom you want to impress. Here are some examples of questions that you should just never, ever ask:

- **"Have you played [highly anticipated game that hasn't been released yet]?"** (Answer: Not unless I worked at that company, or have a very close friend who works there. In either case, I am surely under NDA and am not allowed to talk about it with you.)

- **"Have you played [student game that I made]?"** (Answer: No. I barely get enough time to play all of the games that my industry colleagues have made. I might make an exception if your game won a major award like the IGF Student Showcase, if a lot of other people are talking about it, but that's about it.)

- **"Do you know [famous game developer]?"** (Answer: Maybe I do, maybe I don't. How is this in any way relevant to you having a discussion with me about games?)

- **"I think [Game X] sucks, don't you?"** (Answer: As a professional developer, I know that games often go terribly wrong due to no fault of the talented team that worked on it. This question implies that you do not, and that you have no respect for the hard work that went into a project, and the soul-crushing knowledge that each member of that team has that all their work went to creating a piece of mediocrity. Worse, maybe one of my best friends worked on that game … or maybe I worked on it myself. Maybe I think the game did some really brilliant things that you just failed to notice. Even if I agree with you, the industry is too small for us to slam each other for works that turned out less than we had hoped.)

▪ **"Can I come work for you?"** (Answer: No. If I'm actively hiring and based on our conversation you seem like the kind of person who I'd like to work with, I'll mention it.)

▪ **"What are you working on now; what's it about?"** (Answer: I'm under NDA so I can't say. How about you? Oh, NDA too? Thought so.)

▪ **"Will you look at my game design idea?" / "I have this amazing idea for a game, can I tell you about it?"** (Answer: Most developers have seen so many bad "ideas" that they are sick of it. Even those like me who are less jaded will only do so if we have absolutely nothing better to do at the moment. If it's me you're asking, I'll be happy to look, but note that I will find every conceivable flaw in your design and then some, and you'll only have proven to me just how much further you have to go before you're ready to do this professionally. Furthermore, if you don't have me sign an NDA and then expect to turn around and file a lawsuit of me "stealing" your ideas when the game I'm working on has some tiny resemblance to yours, you can expect to never work in the industry again. If you do ask me to sign an NDA first, the answer is no, I will not sign an NDA just for the privilege of providing you with free advice. On that subject, I also happen to be a design consultant, I charge $60/hour minimum, so expecting me to give you free advice is kind of insulting even if I do agree. At any rate, ideas are just ideas; a better question is "Will you look at my game?" which has most of the same problems, but at least shows me you're capable of putting in some effort to actually make something.)

▪ **"I have this amazing story idea, can I tell you about it?"** (Answer: If you want to write stories, more power to you. I make games. If your story doesn't have gameplay attached, I'm not really interested. You'd be better off talking to someone who writes stories. This also has most of the problems of the previous "I have this amazing idea for a game ..." question.)

Brenda: Ian's answer is inspired. I have nothing to add.

Ian: That's because I wrote this chapter from Brenda's notes, and she forgot about it.

INDEX